MW01142322

WriterLy
→Play←

Transform
Your Teaching
with **Game-Based**
Strategies
and Tools

BY **Naomi Kinsman**

writerly*play*

PLAY. WRITE. REPEAT.

Printed in the USA

First Printing: June 2015

ISBN 978-0-9963450-0-2

www.writerlyplay.com

For MRS. GUINTHER, my first-grade teacher and very first mentor.
Thank you for showing me that each and every person is not like the others.

For GRANDMA GINI, my adopted grandma, who drove me through the
sprinklers with the windows down.
Thank you for helping me find magic in everyday moments.

For MR. ERICKSON, my high-school theatre teacher, who didn't even blink at
the question of how an actor might enter the stage via hot air balloon.
Thank you for teaching me that nearly everything is possible.

And for ANNE URSU, who refused to let me research the importance of play
in other people's creative processes.
Thank you for challenging me to learn to play.

Contents

INTRODUCTION

TAG. YOU'RE IT! It's time to play.

Before we begin, I have to warn you: this book isn't meant to be read in a comfy chair with a highlighter. Dig out your art supplies, sharpen your favorite pencil, and stretch those muscles out. Learning to teach playfully isn't simply a thinking exercise. It's a hands-on, get-what-you-put-into-it, move-around-your-room activity.

When I started developing this book, I sat down with my research, curricula, training materials, and many years of classroom experience rattling around in my brain. I began writing a very scholarly account of what play is, why it matters, and how to make it work in various learning environments. The results were comprehensive and about as playful as wilted spinach.

Here's why I should have known better. During my MFA program, I decided to focus my critical thesis on play and its importance in the creative process. I wanted to refine my teaching experience and shape it into a methodology to share with other educators. Again, I started with the research. Much too quickly, all play disappeared from my life as my desk piled high with studies and academic tomes. What I discovered then is still true today. While the importance of play is backed by volumes of research, an intellectual understanding of this material isn't enough. You need to experience it yourself, as a player.

To that end, I have included playful activities throughout this book. You may be tempted to skip them. Life is busy, after all. I encourage you to resist this urge. Dive into this material, and this experience, as fully as you can. You'll find much value in the playing—value for your writing, for your teaching, and for your students, too. After playing, you'll be able to share firsthand experiences, your successes and—what is infinitely more valuable— your challenges. Your risk taking opens the doorway for your students to do the same.

So what is Writerly Play at heart?

Writerly Play is an approach to developing writing skills. Through games, questions, creative activities, and critical thinking, Writerly Play makes the writing process visible, concrete, and manageable. Writerly Play is a deceptively simple, iterative process that can be repeated and built upon time and time again. The facilitator is a pied piper, a spell weaver, a magician. The games weave a spell to transform a classroom into a playful, filled-with-possibility creative space. Through play, the facilitator opens doorways to discovery, and then lights the way back to practical application on the page. As in the practice of yoga, the more a learner practices the art form, the deeper he or she can go into the experience. Whether you are a classroom teacher, an after-school writing instructor, or a one-on-one mentor, whether you work with developing writers in kindergarten or even adult learners, the Writerly Play process can be adapted to work for you.

This handbook provides games, stories, research, and strategies to guide your Writerly Play journey. Spell weaving is an art form, and one that isn't learned overnight. I can promise that the magic is worth the journey. With practice, you'll have a set of tools with which you can then continue to invent. Play isn't something that can be nailed down or rolled out in a one-size-fits-all manner. That's the fun of Writerly Play. Every writing session becomes a creative challenge, a game played between facilitator and students.

Play for Learning's Sake

As we grow older, we're told play is frivolous. We allow ourselves to indulge in play only when all our other work is done. However, play is an essential part of innovation, progress, and learning. Play transforms the writing process, adding energy, creativity, and the level of growth that can come only from an experimental attitude.

→ THREE-MINUTE BRAIN-STRETCH

Before you dive into this chapter, go open a new document on your computer. Your task is to start a short story on that blank page. Set a timer and work on it for only three minutes. Are you still reading? Stop. Truly, take a few minutes and go write.

How did your writing session go? If you're like most writers, the blank page was formidable. You may not have written any words at all. Take a moment to consider: What makes a blank page so challenging?

Writing is
thinking
made visible.

the CHALLENGE OF THE BLANK PAGE

The blank page never gets easier, no matter how many books you write. Six, sixteen, or sixty-two stories later, beginning a new writing project is like descending a mossy ladder into a cave without a flashlight.

When we face a fresh blank page, who knows what challenges await, or how long the task will take? Unlike math or history, writing is an academic subject that doesn't fit easily into a multiple-choice quiz. In nearly every way, the writing process is filled with the unknown. No wonder we puzzle over how to best help our students develop as writers.

Some educators feel restricted by rubrics that force writing into formulaic, measurable patterns. Others find themselves wandering through daily writers' workshops, unsure whether their students are truly challenging their weak spots and growing as writers. Many avoid teaching writing all together, hoping that exposure to excellent reading material will help students gain writing skill by osmosis.

Writing is a fusion of creative and critical thinking. Idea generation relies heavily on our imaginations. However, growth in writing skill requires analytical thinking, so we must also tap into our systematic, organized minds. Navigating this back-and-forth process is more nuanced than it appears, and most of us have difficulty breaking it down for ourselves, let alone for our students.

Thinking deeply isn't easy. Plus, writing doesn't offer the immediate thrill of a right answer the way a geometry proof might. No wonder many young writers (and educators) groan over writing lessons. Together, they struggle through writing projects without the intrinsic motivation to do the hard work. Any progress made is hard-won and difficult to measure.

The eventual result? Many highly educated adults insist they are not writers, as though being a writer were optional, the way one might choose to be a chef or a car mechanic. Writing is a profession, true, but virtually every profession also requires writing capability. From completing job applications to drafting proposals to writing fundraising letters for our children's school to composing email, nearly every adult puts thoughts into words daily. Not only must we write, we must do so effectively—often persuasively—in order to thrive. The ability to write is a vital life skill.

Thus, we have our puzzle. Writing is an essential subject, it's difficult to teach and assess, and often our students are resistant to the process.

Enter the game.

The reason play is such a natural fit for helping writers develop their skills is that games, by definition, have parameters and challenges. The challenges, in fact, are what make games enjoyable. Imagine tag without any rules. Players would run helter-skelter and tap one another randomly, but no one would be *it*. The players might even end up running away from the playing field altogether.

Instead of beginning my teaching practice with an education degree, my background is in educational and improvisational theatre. As a teaching artist, I visited classrooms with the purpose of educating through the arts. School hours are valuable, so I had to make my time count by blending theatrical instruction with core subjects. Making learning a game became a natural part of my toolkit and teaching style. As I started publishing books for young people, I began offering literacy-focused school visits and residencies.

At first, I used games as a doorway into writing projects, a way to excite young writers about their ideas so they had the motivation to face that terrifying blank page. However, I discovered that well-facilitated games resulted in deeper, more student-driven learning. While playing, students absorbed and applied concepts such as character development or suspense building that would likely have gone over their heads had we discussed them at the white board. Plus, the games offered natural classroom management. The fun of each game kept the class focused and engaged. By strategically directing the flow from game to game, I could also shape the students' overall energy and keep the group moving in a positive, productive direction.

What truly convinced me that play was key to learning writing skill, though, was my master's thesis. My faculty advisor challenged me to try playing as part of my own writing process. I understood the value of the games as a teaching tool, but I soon discovered the deeper value of them as a learner. Games, when I fully engaged in them, helped me see past limitations and unlock otherwise invisible solutions. Instead of agonizing over problems, possibilities leapt to mind. In moments of spontaneous insight, I saw where and why I was stuck. I saw how I could develop my skills further. My own experiences supported what I saw in my classrooms and gathered from the research.

And thus, Writerly Play was born. Writerly Play offers a playful, authentic approach to the process of learning to be a writer. Instead of replacing curriculum, Writerly Play dovetails with many favorite approaches, including Six Traits and Writers Workshop. Educators are encouraged to focus on specific habits their students need to succeed as writers. With the right habits, students have all the tools needed to own their learning process.

The heart of Writerly Play is not any one specific game or activity or rubric. Games become interesting when players give themselves over to the playing, when they let go of trying to recall the rules and simply play. In our classrooms, these moments can become true teaching moments, too. We create this environment by approaching our teaching as play. Yes, there are guidelines and touchstones, but we also have to be open to surprise. When we as facilitators are absorbed in the game, our students can become absorbed, too. At this point, rather than delivering a lesson, teachers and students are collaborating on a learning experience together.

In order to dive into games effectively, and to make in-the-moment decisions about when and how to flow from one game to another, one must intrinsically understand the way individual games work as well as the overall objectives of teaching in this manner. So, I'll pass on to you the challenge my faculty advisor gave me. Along with reading this book, don't forget that the best way to learn to play is to—yep, you've got it—play. Gather a group of peers and try out some of the games in appendix one. If you can, try out an improv class. And take the time to do the more quiet kinds of play suggested in the exercises throughout this handbook. Consider the difference between being a baker who must always have a recipe, and one who can bake by feel. My goal is to help you play by feel so you can translate that intuitive experience into strategies you can practice and apply in your classrooms.

→ **ONE-MINUTE BRAIN-STRETCH**

Where do you get your best ideas? In the shower? In the kitchen while you're cooking? As quickly as you can, brainstorm a list of ten places where inspiration is likely to strike.

Physical movement helps writers enter a state of play.

SETTING *the* STAGE FOR PLAY

"Sometimes when I walk my dog at the end of the day... I will simply walk without thinking, letting my mind roam free. And then I am often given unexpected and beautiful gifts." Madeleine L'Engle, *Walking on Water*

Many artists have stories that echo Madeleine L'Engle's experience, tales of stumbling across the missing piece of a novel while they're digging a hole for a budding tomato plant, or finally understanding what their abstract painting needs while they're wading barefoot through icy waves. When we examine the circumstances surrounding these sudden flashes of inspiration, it turns out that unexpected ideas show up in situations with a few key similarities.

What similarities? Well, walking the dog, gardening, and wading are all physical activities that appeal to the senses; all offer opportunities for deep concentration. Our minds focus on the specifics of the task at hand while our bodies are in motion and physically engaged. Then, our subconscious goes to work. Suddenly, eureka! A spontaneous idea, previously unavailable to us, shows up. Genuine creative play offers this same opportunity. Creating circumstances that allow writers to have these kinds of ideas and artistic discoveries is the purpose of Writerly Play.

Because physical movement is specific and concrete, it helps players navigate between ordinary experience and a state of play. Players can intentionally push themselves to be more physically involved in a game without intellectualizing or analyzing their actions. Therefore, while spontaneity happens subconsciously during creative play, physical activity is a tangible factor. Players can concentrate on physical tasks in order to engage with the game.

While physical activity allows players to begin to play, the rules and challenges of the game engage their minds and allow players to lose themselves in the experience. The more engrossed players become in achieving their tasks, the less aware they are of themselves as players. They lose their self-consciousness and fear of judgment. They avoid analyzing their ideas and impulses. As players focus on the challenges of the game, they have the opportunity for spontaneous response. For our students, this spontaneous response may be a new understanding of how a particular element of story works, or how to blast through a roadblock in their stories. It may be as simple as a new convincing argument for a persuasive essay or an idea for character development. Whatever the discovery, the games allow our writers to make the connections themselves, causing the learning to be more meaningful, more visceral, and longer lasting.

☆ A TYPICAL FIRST DAY ☆

The tension in the air is palpable.

"Writing's not my thing," one student says. Heads nod in agreement.

"No problem," I answer. "Let's play a game. Start by moving around the room. Walk as though you're barefoot on hot sand."

I start to light-foot around the room while they watch me doubtfully. "Go ahead," I encourage. "What might it look like?"

They stand, giving one another that look, the one that says, *I think our teacher might be nuts.*

I keep right on moving, giving the hot sand a few more seconds before moving on to another suggestion, one that requires even less imagination, because I can see this class needs a little encouragement to dive in.

"What might it look like if you were balancing on a beam? Find a line on the carpet and see if you can balance on it."

It's hard to resist a challenge such as this. One after another, students start moving.

"Or what if you were sneaking into the teacher's lounge? What might that look like?"

More join, until the entire class is tiptoeing around the desks.

"And what if a teacher walked in and caught you?" I continue. "How might you walk then? Perfect! That's an I'm-totally-innocent walk if I've ever seen one." I find myself laughing. They're laughing, too. "Now, let's think of another time you might feel guilty. Show me what you might be doing."

After letting them act this out for a moment or two, I call freeze. "Who can tell me what might make a person feel guilty?"

"Sneaking a cookie!" one shouts out.

"Forgetting to bring my homework to school!" another shouts.

"Come on back to the circle," I say, scribbling their ideas on the board. "What if someone tiptoed into a kitchen to sneak some dessert? Who might do such a thing? When might be the worst possible moment to sneak dessert?"

Hands shoot up across the circle before anyone realizes we're writing a story. Soon, we transition back into a game and they each come up with an idea they can't wait to sit down and write. The games have worked their magic.

CONSIDER the BIG PICTURE

Before we discuss a method of teaching, it's important to establish exactly what we're teaching. In essence, writing is transforming thoughts into words on a page.

Learning to write does involve learning a set of skills including spelling, grammar, and organization. Beneath these skills, however, the foundation of writing fiction or nonfiction is the art of thinking well and asking strong questions. In order to help a young writer tackle the challenge of a question such as, "What is the biggest challenge you've faced and what did you learn from it?" in a well-considered way, an instructor must create a safe space. It isn't fair for us to ask students to think deeply and answer honestly if we're not bringing our own best selves to the conversation, too. While we mean well, our own questions and challenges around writing tend to get in our way as teachers. Keeping these concerns unacknowledged often causes them to subconsciously affect our students and their writing.

ASK YOURSELF...

1. When have you felt successful as a writer? What were the circumstances?

2. When have you felt frustrated while writing? What were the circumstances?

3. What do you believe writers need to be successful?

4. What would a class of developing writers look like? Use specifics to set this scene for yourself.

5. What strengths do you bring to the teaching of writing?

6. How would you like to grow as a writing teacher?

So, before we go any further, consider the questions above. Be honest with yourself and give yourself time to free-write your answers.

The Writerly Play method uses games to teach the art of writing. The focus, however, is not on perfect specimens of writing at the end of a unit. The ultimate goal is that students become skillful writers while engaging in the process. While writing today's assignment, they are gaining mastery that they'll need for tackling future writing assignments. They're learning how to ask questions to move past blocks, how to seek answers by studying the writing in their favorite books, and how to choose a strategy to draft and another to revise.

Just as it's tempting—and false—to believe that students who decode well are strong readers, it's tempting—and also false—to believe that capable spellers and students who write perfectly grammatical sentences are strong writers. Their end products may be polished, but what if these students are too afraid to use interesting vocabulary because they don't know how to spell a word? What if they shy away from interesting sentence construction because they don't know how to punctuate it?

Even the most informative writing requires a person to create something that does not yet exist. A writer must string words together in a unique way to express a thought or series of thoughts. While this process does require spelling and grammar, mechanics are hardly the starting point. Still, much of our writing instruction encourages students to begin from just this place. We circle the room and correct misspelled words or confusing sentences to help our young writers learn. Spelling and grammar are the black and white parts of writing, after all, and the easiest

We can inspire students to be writers, to think and invent like writers, to make their words tumble onto the page in their own unique ways.

skills to teach and assess. Thus, our focus is heavily weighted toward these skills. We avoid the more nebulous topics of structure and voice. Our students, for their part, seek the gold-star feeling of a mistake-free piece of writing.

Despite our good intentions, our students learn to construct their writing from a list of words they can easily spell by using the simplest grammar. We become frustrated, wondering why their writing is so rudimentary. We can't put our finger on why they aren't making much progress.

When the focus of writing instruction shifts from a list of dos and don'ts to the joy of sharing one's thoughts on a page, everything changes. Students are motivated to learn how to spell and use grammar because they want to communicate. Be it a story, a letter to Santa, an essay on owls, or a poem, the purpose is always to communicate to the reader. Whether a piece works or not has to do with whether it connects. If the spelling or grammar is unintelligible, it won't connect. The conversation between writer and instructor becomes collegial problem solving. "Hmm... what can we do to make this sentence say exactly what you mean to say? Let's try this strategy..."

I'm not saying that shifting the focus of our teaching is simple. I am saying it's essential. No matter how many games we play, our young writers will never be motivated to improve their skills until they see the purpose and power of their writing. Writing is about communicating ideas, be they imagined places, deeply felt opinions, or our take on interesting facts.

Before we dig into the structure of a Writerly Play lesson and strategies for teaching, in the next chapter, we'll explore the five essential habits of a writer. By focusing on these habits, you'll create a through-line that reminds you and your students of the big picture. Writing tasks are no longer about completing perfect work. They are about practicing writerly habits. Some pieces will be developed to completion. Others are just exercises. All count toward the larger goal of inspiring your students to claim their identity as writers.

FIRST...

Imagine yourself running into one of your students a few years down the road. What if he or she remembered a moment from one of your writing lessons and recounted the experience. In an ideal world, how might the encounter go? Write a short scene bringing the dream scenario to life.

AND THEN...

After you write your scene, reflect on how the writing went for you. Was it easy to write with the amount of guidance given? Difficult? What challenges did you face going from prompt to the blank page? Did you take risks? Did you try to write perfectly? Did you rush through the exercise so you could go on to the next chapter? What insight does your own reaction give you about your students' experience?

DON'T MISS OUT ON THE GOOD STUFF! GIVE YOURSELF TIME TO WRITE AND REFLECT. WHEN YOU DO, YOU'LL GET MORE OUT OF WRITERLY PLAY. I PROMISE!

CHAPTER TWO

Writerly Habits

Similar to becoming a gymnast, a violinist, or a chef, becoming a writer involves internalizing skills learned through regular practice. We'd never expect a cooking newbie to enter a kitchen alone and succeed, even with a recipe. New chefs must learn to measure and chop and, most importantly, to think about the big picture. In the same way, writers need to learn writerly habits to prepare for the blank page.

Walk through your house and collect five objects that connect to your interests or remind you of meaningful experiences. Hold each in turn, and think of one specific story the object conjures. Close your eyes and see each memory as a movie, frame by frame.

Write what you know...with a twist.

the WRITER'S SUITCASE

The Suitcase

The first writerly habit is collecting inspiration from our everyday lives. We have suitcases that fill every hour, every week with sights, sounds, textures, and memories. Ultimately, this collection fuels our writing.

Educators debate about whether students learn enough from writing fiction to devote valuable class time to such projects. Often the emotional heart of a story is missing when students jump into a story about pirates or aliens or hot air balloons. The farther the topic from the author, the less the author connects authentic emotions with the characters. In a magical world, cause and effect is often swapped out for random strokes of the supernatural. Settings become wonky or nonexistent, and world-building rules are made and broken.

However, walk into any classroom and tell the students that today they're going to imagine a story and then write it. The entire room will light up. There's magic in the invitation to create a story beyond the confines of one's everyday life. Every once in a while, a child will play it safe and write facts or a story from his or her life, but the majority will dive into fiction with a passion they'd never bring to other writing tasks.

We know that learning is exponentially greater when a student is intrinsically motivated to do a task. So, think of the power fiction has to help kids learn to write. Fiction is fun, naturally motivating, and requires nearly all of the skills that other writing requires. I'm not saying nonfiction can't be fun, nor that students don't enjoy writing about topics of deep interest to them. However, here too, the beginnings of motivation come from the students' sense of wonder and curiosity. Questions such as "What if..." and "How does..." fuel these writing projects. The surest way to quash this passion is to force an entire class to write on a narrowly focused topic that appeals only to a few. Or worse, to use writing primarily as a test to gauge learning. When students write to prove their knowledge, the joy of exploration, of trying to share their ideas and questions, disappears.

If our goal is to tap into students' passion and inspire them to write from their hearts, fiction is an excellent vehicle. Still, we have the difficulty of the messy, disconnected stories that often show up. How can we bridge this gap?

Understanding the Suitcase

When I explain the Suitcase to a new group of students, I bring along an actual suitcase with artifacts from my life. I may include a photo of my family on vacation, a medal from a half-marathon, a set of drawing pencils, and a certificate from my black bear course. I show each, and explain how these experiences provide me with writing material.

Depending on the writing unit's focus, I explain how, though these items point to factual events in my life, I can also use them to form fiction. I might discuss how after my black bear course, I knew more about wild-bear behavior. I learned about the issues caused by humans and black bears living in close quarters. Using that knowledge, I was able to set my fictional Sadie's Sketchbook series in a town with wild black bears living nearby.

While it is true that we gather items in our Suitcase unknowingly and throughout every day, part of this habit is to pay attention to those items, to gather and examine them, and to consider how they might transform into story material. Thus, the Suitcase isn't only about having experiences, but about collecting them, too.

Our Writerly Play workbooks include a Suitcase section in which writers can collect their life experiences with more intention, through questions and activities. However, even if your writers aren't working with an official Writerly Play workbook, encourage them to create a physical

space for their Suitcase. It may be an actual suitcase or a section of their journal, binder, or online notebook. The idea is that writers will collect ideas here and examine those thoughts over time, allowing interesting connections to be made among the various events of their lives. Those connections create sparks that flare into fresh writing material.

☆ TAPPING EXPERTISE ☆

"I'm not an expert at anything," she insists, throwing her pencil down.

I crouch beside her desk. "When we were playing Choices, you moved to the side of the room for 'having a big family.' Do you have a lot of brothers and sisters?"

"Brothers," she says. "Three of them. I'm the oldest."

"Would you say you're an expert at being a big sister?"

"Like, how?" she asks.

"I'm not sure. I'm an only child. But I imagine that you've worked out how to get out of trouble when someone tattles. Or maybe how to play practical jokes? Or probably how to sneak away and get some alone time."

A smile tips the corner of her mouth upward. "Yeah. I guess I'm pretty good at those things."

"What if your character was a big sister?"

"She'd have to build a tree house to get away from her brothers," she says, picking up her pencil.

I stay as she starts to write, but after a moment, I see that she doesn't need me even a little anymore. She's off and running. After all, she is the expert.

→ A SUITCASE COOLDOWN

Look back over the objects you collected from around your house. How might you use objects in your Suitcase as sparks for fiction? Using the sentence starter "I could write about...," brainstorm at least three quick story ideas that tap into your expertise.

Draw a T-chart in your notebook. On one side, list the writing skills about which you feel confident. On the other side, list areas where you feel you could grow. If you get stuck, use the list of writing skills in appendix two as a starting place.

Focus on one skill at a time.

the WRITER'S WORKSHOP

The second writerly habit is building skills, one at a time. Just as we might learn to use a hammer, and saw to build a table, as writers we develop a set of tools that allow us to wrangle new writing challenges.

Over time, I found that young writers basically fit into one of two categories: stuck or moving so fast that they didn't stop to think. Neither was ideal, given my goal of helping them grow as writers. If writers were stuck, their focus was on the lack of ideas. When in motion, they focused on what would happen next. My question was: How might I shift the students' focus to character motivation or descriptive language or creating suspense?

As an educator, I was committed to doing more than providing students with drafting time and space to find their own way. I wanted to help them focus on developing their skills with intention. However, as a writer, I realized that during the drafting process, we often do write in a mad rush and then return to fix problems later. With student writers there are a few difficulties with this mad-rush drafting process. First, most young writers don't have the energy or inclination to go back and revise their drafts unless they are forced to do so. At that point, revision

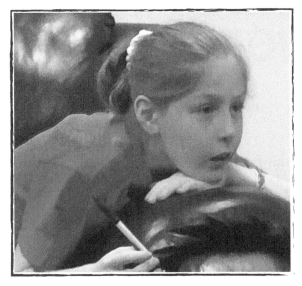

becomes a battleground. Changes tend to focus on spelling and word choice, rather than more complex questions such as structure or point of view. Another issue with unfocused drafting is that it often means practicing bad habits. Instead of adding skills slowly over time and practicing them, a young writer develops a piece with whatever prior knowledge he or she already possesses. Then, when it is time to revise, our writers learn several new skills. With this advanced perspective, they look back over their pieces and feel disappointed with their work. Disappointed and weary from the work already completed, they resist fixing their pieces. Instead, they want to start over, and thus begin the cycle of first-draft writing again.

The part of my artist-brain that loves a puzzle went to work on this conundrum. If I didn't want to interrupt the drafting process, but I also wanted to ensure that young writers are learning along the way, how could I help them? One on one, this problem was easier to tackle, as we could identify a skill particularly relevant to the day's writing and discuss that topic to launch our work together. For the class as a whole, however, a different strategy was required. So, I started using mini-lessons at the top of each writing session. Each mini-lesson focused on one isolated writing skill that a student could consider in regard to his or her story. Since we played a game around that skill, or completed a playful worksheet, or both, writers had a chance to think about the skill outside their stories. Then, after watching me model how to apply that skill to a story, students had the opportunity to write. Some writers, the linear ones, applied what we had just explored right away. However, many filed the information away and used it later, when the particular skill came up again in their stories. In this way, we could address the various parts of story development and learn session by session as a group.

Understanding the Workshop

The Workshop helps the facilitator and the young writers focus on specific skills within their writing while ignoring everything else. When focusing on dialogue, for instance, we may lose track of descriptive writing all together. The unspoken agreement is that while character, setting, plot, word choice, sentence structure, tone, point of view, and so on, are always important while writing a story, the best way to improve is to focus on one specific area at a time. The topic might be using habitual gesture to show emotion or establishing mood through the narrator's word choice. The narrower the focus, the more likely that young writers will gain a strategy that they can use over time.

→ A WORKSHOP COOLDOWN

Look back over the list of writing skills you made at the beginning of this section. Choose one area in which you might grow. For that area, brainstorm and choose one specific activity you might practice or one resource you might consult. If time allows, go try the activity or find the resource now!

→ FIVE-MINUTE BRAIN-STRETCH

Flip through an old magazine and tear out images that catch your attention. After your five minutes are up, look over the collection. What kind of character might the pictures inspire? A gardener who wishes she could travel to Venice? A chef who has fallen head over heels in love?

Especially if this is a new approach for you, notice how starting from a fresh entry point affects your idea-generation process.

At best, problem solving can be a game.

the WRITER'S STUDIO

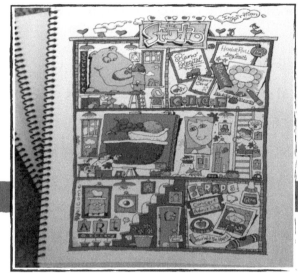

The third writerly habit is to brainstorm playfully. Picture an art studio filled with colorful supplies, where artists explore options. To develop ideas, solve problems, and innovate, writers must experiment, too.

Take any theatre game, boil it down to its basics, and you'll find a problem in need of a solution. Actors often improvise ways to solve problems on the fly, and soon become adept at coming up with multiple solutions for any given challenge. Instead of cowering behind excuses, many actors have a "let's try it" attitude.

One reason games are such a rich resource for writers is that while we play, a rich invisible alchemy is taking place in our minds. Through playing, we discover there is not only one solution to the puzzle we're working out in the story, but potentially many. While wrestling through a stubborn block, most of us would not believe this reality if someone explained it to us. However, discovered for ourselves, and in an engaging way, the truth can't be ignored.

Successful writers are problem solvers. Sooner or later, we all come up against a creative question that has the power to freeze us in our tracks. Maybe we realize a character isn't as real as she once seemed, or that we're starting to write in a formulaic way. Maybe we write ourselves into a corner and can't see a path to a realistic conclusion. At these moments, we must decide whether we will actively seek solutions or make excuses. If we're veteran game players, with hours of experiences that prove to us that solutions are at our fingertips, we're much better off.

Writers need to practice brainstorming playfully. Whether ideas are flowing or not, we should keep ourselves in good shape so that when our ideas dry up, we have the courage and problem-solving chops to dig deep and find solutions. Once students gain these skills in our Writerly Play workshops, they can practice on their own, even if they aren't with a class full of other writers and a facilitator to guide them through a game. A game need only have a physical component and some rules to define the creative boundaries. Designing a collage can be a game, particularly if you give yourself a time limit within which to work. Listing twenty items to put into a scene is a game, and particularly so if you write in large letters on a whiteboard or easel or in sidewalk chalk on your front porch, getting your whole body into it. Large movement or small, huge or simple challenge, it's the playing that's important.

Understanding the Studio

The Studio provides open-ended prompts and activities to help writers brainstorm. Also, the Studio offers space for writers to collect ideas. Many writers find that when they start writing, the creative momentum rattles loose new ideas. Often these unexplored ideas are more attractive than the ones in which we're knee-deep. It's easy to fear losing our ideas if we don't drop everything and work on them immediately. Using the Studio to collect ideas helps writers focus on one project at a time, and also honors the way creativity shows up. Some days are just more inspired than others. When we value that flow of ideas by capturing it in words and images, we make it more likely that another day full of inspiration will come.

One strategy that is useful to explore with writers in the Studio is the mind map. A mind map or sketchnote is a collection of words and images designed to explore and communicate an idea. Mind maps and sketchnotes can be as simple as a spiderweb diagram or much more fully illustrated. Whether young writers use stick figures or more complex drawings, the more colorful and playful a mind map, the better. Help your writers practice gathering a wealth of ideas— more than they need—and watch them gain the resilience they'll require for days when they're blocked.

⇥ A STUDIO COOLDOWN

Gather a wealth of ideas for yourself! Give yourself a few more minutes to look through that magazine and make a page or two of idea-sparking collages to add to your Studio.

→ **THREE-MINUTE BRAIN-STRETCH**

Take a book you love off the shelf. Set a timer for three minutes, and list everything you appreciate about the book. You'll find you start with more general thoughts and then drill down to more specific ones as you continue. Challenge yourself to keep that pencil moving.

Writers who read closely become self-directed learners.

the WRITER'S LIBRARY

The Library

The fourth writerly habit is to read thoughtfully. After noticing how our favorite authors create tension or develop characters, we can use those same strategies as tools in our own writing toolkits.

Once a writer can identify an effect he or she is trying to create and finds an example of that effect in a book, a world of possibility opens up. Every book is a potential teacher, every reading experience an opportunity to inspire. While we as instructors can continue to help students see their blind spots, as thoughtful readers, students become empowered to identify their own areas of growth as well.

Even very young writers can begin to learn this skill. In many kindergarten or first-grade classrooms, students create class books in the style of a published story, such as *Cloudy with a Chance of Meatballs*. In this way, students are stepping into a published author's shoes and trying a new approach to writing they may not have thought of by themselves. With slightly older students, we often see fan fiction in which a young writer immerses him or herself in the world of someone else's story. Fan fiction writers may create a new plot by inserting a new character into the setting or even by inserting themselves into the world of the story. For instance, a student might write a "What Would Happen to Me in Narnia" story. While students naturally transfer some qualities or topics from their reading to their writing, the art of reading as a writer is a habit that must be developed. To read as writers, we must pull back from the reading experience and think analytically about how an author shaped his or her story.

Here's how the process might look. First we ask: What's successful about this story? Then: Which of those qualities would I like to focus on? Then: Where do I see the author achieving that quality? Finally: After reading this passage, what strategy can I take away for my own writing? How might I try out that strategy?

To make this level of deep reading possible, we must model the process for our students. First, we might read a passage to highlight an author's approach. For instance, if our focus was introducing secondary characters, we might read a few paragraphs that show a character's entrance. Books are also a great addition to conferring sessions.

Keep in mind that we're not asking our students to stop reading as readers and to start always reading as writers. First, we read for joy. Then, we can reread to learn why a book works so well. Reading thoughtfully isn't meant to make reading into a chore. If we can show our students how to read deeply in specific sections of a book (identified later because we've read the whole thing and enjoyed it already), they'll be much more willing to do the tough thinking required to mine their favorite books for those gems they can apply to their own work.

Understanding the Library

If you use a Writerly Play workbook in your classroom, you'll have access to a variety of Library worksheets. Some of these are more structured, and others are more open-ended, to appeal to various learning and thinking styles. In the resources section on the Writerly Play website, we also have a sample set of Library worksheets that you can download and use. We find that adapting the questions to focus on the genre of book or skill in question helps readers drill down to specifics as they analyze the books they love. Thus, we encourage you to adapt accordingly, based on your unique needs.

Reading thoughtfully isn't as naturally appealing as brainstorming playfully or collecting inspiration—it requires more focused critical thinking. However, by modeling how to use the Library, we help young writers take greater charge of their learning and help them learn to use resources they know well to shape their own writerly development.

→ A LIBRARY COOLDOWN

Review the list of qualities you appreciate about your chosen book. Look for a passage that is a strong example of that quality. Then, consider how the author has achieved the quality. If you were to transform this effect into a strategy, what would you call it? What would the steps be?

→ **FIVE-MINUTE BRAIN-STRETCH**

Using the character you developed from the Studio collage or another character of your choice, write a quick scene. Put the character in a setting in which he or she would feel comfortable, and then introduce a problem. How does your character go about solving the problem?

Thinking about writing isn't the same as actually writing.

the WRITER'S DEN

The fifth writerly habit is to write regularly. Similar to painting or playing the piano, writing is a practice that one must develop. Over time, our concentration and creativity grow stronger and easier to access.

Ask any writer and he or she will tell you: Thinking about writing isn't the same as writing. Learning about writing isn't the same as writing. Even planning our writing isn't the same as writing. The thing is, writers have to actually write. And while this may seem obvious, the truth is that writers of all ages come up with a plethora of ingenious ways to avoid writing. We sharpen pencils, look up interesting character names, research locations, make playlists for our characters...but we don't write.

The greatest gift we can give our young writers is the time, space, and encouragement to sit down and write. No matter our age, the more often we put down word after word, the more stamina and skill we gain.

It's important to make building stamina a challenge that students want to tackle. By making writers aware that they are building their ability to stick with the process, we help them see that writing stamina doesn't tend to be a natural gift. Everyone can improve this skill with practice. Maybe to begin, our students can write for three minutes straight. The next day, they might be able to write for four. Or five. If need be, we can provide external motivation for building stamina, such as stickers or games as rewards, but ultimately we want accomplishing the challenge to be its own reward.

Understanding the Den

The Den is the mental space we enter when we close out the world and craft words into sentences on the page. Whether we're writing a story, an essay, a poem, or a report, we're drawing on the full tank of strategies and ideas we've created through practicing all the other habits. For most writers, the Den is a place where analytical thinking fades into the background and we submerge ourselves in the flow of creation. Rather than focusing on which skill we're using or analyzing every word choice, in the Den we draw upon our collection of skills and—in the best writing sessions—using those skills subconsciously.

It's important not to become so busy with the other habits that we forget to apply them to real-world writing. Remember, thinking about writing and writing aren't the same thing. In order to model the writing process for our students, we must be able to share real-life stories about our own questions, discoveries, and struggles. Ideally, as instructors, we write both in and out of class. Outside class, we can have a true writing experience that isn't interrupted by our need to monitor our students. Outside class writing helps us remember what it feels like to write, helps us develop our writing skills, and gives us stories from the trenches to share with our students.

Inside class, when writing time begins, I also try to take a few minutes to write before working with students. This investment of a few minutes has a couple important benefits. First, this time gives me a bit of writing to share with my students, should I choose to do so. Sometimes, while applying our mini-lesson of the day, I realize there's a question I should address for the group using my thinking or writing as an example. In some classes, my story becomes an example that builds session after session. My students and I can then discuss applying skills in the nonthreatening environment of my work rather than their own. The other reason I write first and then confer is because this flow forces students to try to apply the day's lesson on their own before I step in to help. This way, I give them space in which to struggle—just a bit—which helps build self-sufficiency. Soon, my students realize they are more capable writers than they first believed, which is one of the most valuable discoveries they can make.

→ A DEN COOLDOWN

Block out fifteen minutes each day this week. During that time, open up your journal and write. Start with a character, a setting, and a problem. For fun, enlist friends or family members to give you suggestions, the way audiences give actors ideas for improv scenes. Improvise until the timer rings. That's it. After the week is up, review. How does it feel to write regularly?

FIRST...

Take out a set of colored pencils or markers and a white sheet of paper. Using color, sketches, and hand-drawn words, brainstorm a space you might make for each of the writerly habits. I like using a set of journals, one per habit. Others like using a binder. Some use a shelf, a box, and a diary. Whichever tool works best for you, that's the one to use.

AND THEN...

Once you've completed your colorful brainstorm, make those five physical spaces—one per habit—and put at least one item into each. A list, a brainstorm, an image, a quote, a goal...if you're not sure where to start, simply create labels for each space. Use those colored pencils or pens and let loose a bit. Yes, allow yourself to add a doodle here and there. Cut out some pictures or add some glitter. Whatever you do, give yourself the space to have fun.

A Lesson's Flow

———◆———

In Writerly Play workshops, games and activities are orchestrated to create an effective flow. Just as games create limitations that allow learners to relax and play, a trustworthy pattern to the overall lesson provides facilitators with needed structure. This structure allows them to adapt and play their way through the day's instruction.

The White Queen encouraged Alice to believe six impossible things before breakfast. Why? I think because belief begets belief. Try this: List six examples of things that you once thought impossible that came to be. Maybe you learned to do something you at first believed you couldn't do. Perhaps you were in a play and a few days before opening night, everyone was positive the performance would never come together. The more examples you remember, the more you'll start to wonder what's actually stopping us most of the time: our

doubt, or our reality?

Here's the secret sauce: belief. We believe, and so our students grow to believe too.

FIRST THINGS FIRST

More than the games, more than the lesson structure, more than our expertise, more than anything, really—what makes Writerly Play work are our positive expectations.

When we believe our students can find a solution to their creative challenges, even the T. rex-sized obstacles can be overcome. We believe, and so our students grow to believe, too. Notice I said "grow to believe"? This confidence is not a first-day, first-experience kind of thing. Learning to play takes time, particularly when one has built a wall around his or her creative heart. Brick by brick, the wall must come down.

Before discounting this work as too difficult, consider the crippling thoughts those bricks represent: *Nothing important happens in my life. I don't have any stories to tell. I can't spell. My teacher hates dinosaurs. Imagination won't get me into college. Beetle-birds? What a dumb idea. Playing is just for little kids—I should grow up!*

Regardless of how much we want to solve problems for our students, we must allow them to discover their own answers.

Beliefs such as these only grow in power when left to fester. Absolutely, we're helping students learn to write, but there's something larger going on in our workshops. We're clearing the way for possibilities. We're helping students learn to ask *What if...?* rather than ruminate on the roadblocks. As we move past everything that's in the way, students start writing from their hearts. Without meaning to, they realize *Homelessness really bothers me—What else can I do to help?* Or, *I guess I'm more upset about not being cast in the play than I thought. Maybe I should talk to the director.* Or *I never really thought about things from Alison's point of view. Maybe I should try talking to her about our fight again.*

Here, we come to the heart of why teaching writing is so difficult—and so meaningful. We're journeying into the land of ideas and beliefs and emotion. It's a place of profound vulnerability. No wonder the claws come out—and not just on the part of our students. Consider the fight or flight response we battle through to sit with a friend after he or she has experienced a loss. Being present is terrifying. We might say the wrong thing or do the wrong thing. We definitely won't have all the answers.

So, how do we honestly believe no obstacle is too large when we know we won't have all the answers? There's the paradox. As facilitators, we can't expect to provide every solution, but what we can bring to the conversation is actually more powerful—an infinite number of questions. Questions provide new perspective on sticky problems. Instead of rushing in with a canned answer that would likely feel unsatisfying to our students, we can help them find a question that leads to another and then to another. When writers are exploring questions rather than obsessing over roadblocks, they can dismantle their own walls.

Remember when I said this process is iterative? Skills develop, of course, but no matter how many books we have written, writers must practice, over and over and over. As facilitators, we carve out a possibility-filled space in which risk-taking is possible.

How?

1. First, we *listen* and *provide perspective*.

2. Then, we *encourage playful exploration*.

3. Next, we help writers *apply their playful discoveries* to the project at hand. These practical strategies lead into writing, and thus the circular process continues.

THE WRITERLY PLAY PROCESS

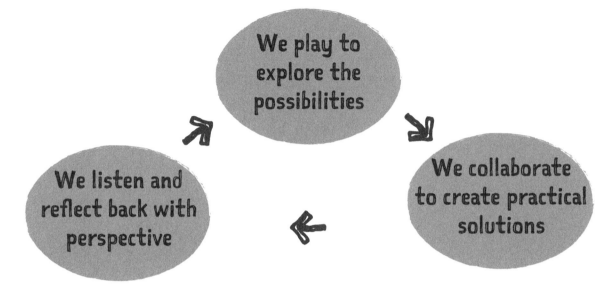

This perspective-play-practical strategies conversation is the foundation for every Writerly Play lesson, be it one-on-one or with a larger group. When writing momentum lags, facilitators need only locate themselves in relation to this conversation and determine: What do we need next?

PERSPECTIVE? Do we need to discuss what's happening and identify a challenge or multiple challenges to tackle?

PLAY? Is it time to move away from talking and thinking into a more abstract, creative space in which we can experiment and explore?

PRACTICAL SOLUTIONS? Have we created a tornado of creative energy that now needs to touch down in a manageable form on the page?

☆ CHARACTERS COMING OUT MY EARS ☆

"I can't write the scene! There are too many people. It's all over the place—everyone is talking and I'm totally confused."

She's curled up on the couch, staring hopelessly into her computer. I especially want to help her past this hurdle. She's been drafting this book for months now. I don't want this scene to defeat her.

Hopeful, I ask, "Are you sure you need all of the characters in the scene?"

"She's supposed to feel overwhelmed because there are all these kids, they're all friends, and she's new." She shakes her head. "So yes, they're all important."

I see the wall she's facing as clearly as if it were a tangible thing sitting between us in the room. I'm tempted to push her on this point. Of course she *could* take out some of the characters, and it *would* make the scene easier to write, but she's making an artistic choice, being true to her intent for the scene. She doesn't need me to solve this for her; she needs me to help her believe she can find a solution for herself.

"So they're all talking at the same time?"

"Well, not exactly. It's more like they disappear and then suddenly reappear when they toss a comment into the conversation. I can't keep reminding the reader they're all there without listing their names over and over."

"So maybe it would help if we play with the scene a different way. What if we tried to stage it like a play?" I take out colored pencils and a piece of paper. "Can you draw the room? Just an eagle's-eye diagram?"

"Umm... Well, they're all at this big table." She draws a rectangle and starts to draw smaller squares for chairs.

"You're frowning."

"Yeah. It's boring," she says. "I mean, what group of teenagers sits around a big table to hang out?"

"Where else could they be?"

"I don't know, maybe on couches and...yeah, lounging on pillows. All around a fire." She flips the paper over and starts sketching furiously, noting where each character would be in relation to the others. When she finishes, she looks up at me. "Okay, now what?"

"You need them to talk to each other, right?"

"Yeah, but how do I keep it from becoming a mess again?"

"What do you need the scene to do? What kinds of things need to happen, other than a bunch of kids talking to one another?"

"She needs to get to know the others. And Julien, he needs to posture, make himself bigger than the others. And Rachel needs to be the practical one. Kato needs to clown around."

"Could they do those things with action? What else could be happening besides just talking? What would you do in the evening with a group of your friends?"

"Eating snacks, for sure. And playing games, maybe. They could be playing a card game."

"Perfect. What if you write it out as a scene with dialogue and action?"

And she's off.

What she needed was a playful way to look at her problem. She needed a sandbox in which to try out a what-if. Imagine we rewind this scene. Had I asked her to try out a mental what-if, she'd likely have obsessed over coming up with the perfect idea. Had I asked her to start freewriting something new, she'd probably have started from the table and quickly become convinced she'd never fix the scene. The solution wasn't in the activity—in this case staging the scene—but more in the opportunity that imagining the scene as a play provided. With room to experiment, to discover what wasn't working, she found her own solution. As a bonus, she built her confidence about fixing future problems, too.

→ FIVE-MINUTE BRAIN-STRETCH

Set a timer for three minutes and make a list of games you remember playing as a child. Then, choose one that is particularly compelling. Maybe you had forgotten about playing that game; or as you wrote it down, a particular face, image, or sensory memory came to mind. Take two minutes or so to visualize yourself playing the game. Bring to mind any sensory details that you can, particularly scent and sound, as these are the most evocative for memory. If sketching, listing or freewriting will better help you visualize, then use those tools. Ask yourself: What environment made play most possible for me?

Plan each lesson with a few guidelines plus a basic structure. Then...play!

ORCHESTRATING A LESSON

Your teaching toolkit is packed with your improvisational spirit, your teaching objective, and your plans to listen, play, and strategize. Now what?

You have a writer or a classroom of writers staring at you (or possibly clowning around the room). To approach this creative challenge as a game, we need a few guidelines and a basic structure from which to improvise. How might an ideal Writerly Play lesson go?

To begin, let's unpack a typical group lesson. This template also serves as the foundation for one-on-one mentoring sessions, but group lessons tend to stick more closely to this format. In groups, a more structured approach allows us to wrangle multiple personalities and address varying needs of individual learners. In after-school situations with only one session per week, we recommend no more than twelve young writers per instructor. This allows one-on-one conferring time for all students. However, Writerly Play methods work well in regularly sized school classrooms as well. With multiple writers' workshop sessions through the week, there

A TYPICAL LESSON

1. The Invitation

2. The Connection

3. The Mini-Lesson

4. Modeling

5. Writing/Conferring

6. Sharing

7. Casting a Line

is time to cycle through brief student conferences every few days.

The Invitation

The invitation sparks curiosity at the top of a lesson. When students arrive, the facilitator assesses the group and decides how best to transition the class into a focused, energized, creative state. Effective invitations quickly highlight the session's learning objective in an entertaining way.

If students will trickle in for your Writerly Play lesson, you may want your invitation to begin with independent work. This way, you focus writers' attention as the group slowly gathers.
If your students are all present, but not ready to focus on the opening ritual, use a game to help them transition.

End your invitation with an opening ritual. This intentional activity has an element of predictability that will help you and your young writers transform the classroom into a creative space. Ideally, develop a ritual that can change and morph over time so you can add variety and additional complexity as your writerly community develops.

PICTURE THESE TWO SCENARIOS

In the first scenario, kids stream into the classroom, laughing and shoving. They throw their backpacks down just anywhere, creating various stumbling blocks in the playing space. Some perch on desks, others flop into the reading-corner couch, and three girls launch into a pillow fight. Two boys come through the door one after the other, wearing identical scowls. They're not looking at each other and slouch into chairs on opposite sides of the room.

It's time for class to start, so you say, "Okay, today we're going to develop our main characters. Everyone up, let's play!"

Maybe two of the twelve students stand up and you have to cajole the rest to un-plaster themselves from their seats. By the time everyone is finally standing up, half the class has dissolved into a joke-off, and you can't hear yourself think.

In the second scenario, you greet kids at the door. You show them where to put their bags down and walk them to the circle. You give them a thinking or quiet discussion activity while you finish catching stragglers. Then, when everyone is present, you turn out the lights and bring a flashlight to the circle. Opening a leather-bound book of poems, you read by flashlight, passing the book and flashlight around the circle so each student can participate by reading the poem line-by-line.

Closing the book's cover, you point out the mysterious tone of this particular poem, and explain that the kids will be writing their own mysteries in this workshop. And they'll be creating their stories by playing games. To demonstrate, you play a quick question-and-answer game in which they get to know one another better. Then, you provide a few ground rules, flip the light on and say, "Everyone up, let's play!"

Which of these two scenarios would you prefer? Probably the second, though you might worry about all the class time this sequence would burn. The truth is, though, eliminating the transition time caused by disorder and chaos with a well-orchestrated opening actually saves time. Better still, writers are primed to soak in more, to transition into play more quickly, and to trust you more.

So what does a strong opening ritual look like? It's an activity that gathers the writers into a circle and focuses their energy. Opening rituals work best when they are familiar. The spell they weave becomes more powerful as they are repeated in lesson after lesson. Still, slight variations can and should be added to keep things interesting. For instance, if the ritual is a sentence-by-sentence invention of a story, each week the group prompt should be different.

The purpose of the invitation is to create a doorway through which you and your writers can dependably travel into a productive session.

The Connection

The invitation leads directly to the connection. Think of the connection as a big, red "You Are Here" marker. In the same way a complex map becomes clear when we locate ourselves, the learning landscape sharpens when students tap into their prior, connected knowledge. *Ah,* they think, *I know about creating characters. I see where we might go with this.*

A connection might be a question, a statement, or a discussion. It links today's learning objective to the topic explored in the last session or to the writers' experiences outside this workshop.

Just as a writer carefully adds basic information to a first page of a story to ground his or her readers, facilitators do the same in their sessions. The purpose here is to remove confusion and help learners gain an overall vision for the learning they are about to experience.

Keep in mind: As a facilitator, you walk a fine line between providing a magical experience for your class and seeming to BE magic. Providing context and helping students set their own objectives for the learning process gives them ownership. They are empowered to think, make decisions, and ask

Leave room for your students to make magic of their own.

their own questions. This way, they won't fall into the trap of believing they can't create unless you're around.

The Mini-Lesson

The mini-lesson often consists of one to three short games that focus on and explore the topic of the day. Sometimes, depending on the learning styles and writing ability of your group, you may decide to begin the mini-lesson with a white-board demonstration. For instance, rather than starting with a game to explore using action to show emotion, you might discuss how this concept works in words and sentences first. Then, with stronger direction about what the game will help them achieve, writers can play to explore the concept further. In general, I find that younger groups do better starting with the game. Older, more experienced groups can go either way. Sometimes too much setup discussion causes players to over-think the game. Choose your format based on what you feel will most help your writers stretch their skills.

The idea of the mini-lesson is to go deeply into one sharply focused topic. Since each writer and each piece of writing is unique, it would be false to think that on the first day of class everyone would need to develop character; on the second, a setting; and on the third, a plot. Stories don't pack into neat boxes in that way. If a mini-lesson addresses dialogue and a writer isn't ready to add dialogue that day, no big deal. He or she can tuck the information away until it is needed.

Stories are made up of many moving parts, so any given writer in your group may be thinking about five or even twelve different aspects of their story while they play the mini-lesson games.

As the facilitator, however, we must focus on our objective. Even though there are thousands of decisions involved with creating a character, we make the process more manageable by turning our attention to one decision at a time. For instance, we might use a session to examine the contents of our character's pockets. What does this information tell us about the character? Students will own this strategy going forward, now able to use it and apply it in other situations.

Don't be afraid to name your learning objective for the writers. This, again, is about helping students own their learning. You're drawing back the curtain and letting them peek at the inner workings of a process that might otherwise seem enigmatic. We want to help our students develop beyond the theory that, in order for them to write well, it has to be one of those days when lightning strikes.

Modeling

The games create piles of thoughts and ideas, but sometimes that positive energy turns to confusion when we sit down to write. It can feel like taking out a bunch of art materials, arranging everything, and then freezing. So much is available, but where will we start? Modeling helps students find a starting place so they can transform ideas into words on the page.

When we model, we think aloud, weigh options, talk through our reasoning, and ultimately make decisions. Modeling takes a variety of forms including:

A THINK-ALOUD, in which the facilitator composes in the moment on a white board, using the skill discussed in the lesson.

A SHORT READING that demonstrates the skill in finished writing.

A PENCIL AND PAPER ACTIVITY, in which students experiment with the skill.

Our Writerly Play workbooks are very useful during the modeling portion of the lesson. If you don't use our workbooks for your sessions, consider creating a set of worksheets to help focus your students' thinking as they bridge from the activity of the day into the writing. We recommend that you provide a variety of worksheet options which will appeal to those writers who need more space for open brainstorming, and those who need more structured lists of questions. When we design our workbooks, we consider how to facilitate thinking for structured as well as creative thinkers. Whenever I present a new workbook to a class of writers, I point out that like the games, worksheets are tools. They aren't meant to be prescriptive, and if they don't match exactly with the writer's ideas, then part of the game is adapting the questions so they do. Adapting might mean reframing the question—*What shoes does your character wear* becomes *what do your dragon's claws look like*. Sometimes adapting a question means realizing that this question doesn't apply for our story—*what kind of pet would your character have or want to have* leads the writer to

☆ IS IT OKAY IF...? ☆

"Wait!" he calls from across the room. "Is it okay if my character doesn't wear shoes?"

"Freeze!" I say, halting the rest of the group in their tracks. "This is a question you'll think often in this class. My answer to 'Is it okay if...?' is always yes, unless the idea puts you or others in danger. As we keep playing, if this question pops into your mind, I want you to tell yourself, 'Yes, yes, that's okay.' and then keep playing. That way, we don't have to interrupt each other and we can all adapt for our own story's special needs."

"My character is a bear, so he has paws," the boy says.

"Fantastic! Here's the other thing. Instead of making yourself crawl as a bear, consider the kind of movement the bear would have. As though you're an actor on two feet, playing a bear. The word, 'lumber' comes to mind. Try being a bear without crawling, so you can get a sense of what it would feel like to move in the way a bear might move. Okay? Let's move."

discover *My character would hate animals of all kinds! She'd particularly despise birds and go out of her way to avoid them.*

One note on skipping questions, however. Often we avoid a question because it touches a hot spot. Sometimes resistance means that question is the very one we need to answer. When I see young writers writing "no, no, no" on line after line of their worksheets, I stop them and do an impromptu one-on-one character interview.

It may be that this student is not a worksheet sort of person. Often in these cases, he or she has developed the habit of passively resisting teachers by doing the very minimum on handouts. In these cases, remind the writer that no one is grading these worksheets. Maybe give an example of how an unexpected question may have helped you in your writing process.

On the other hand, the writer's story may be untraditional enough that he or she needs different guiding questions. In this case, brainstorming adaptations that will work may solve the problem.

Writing/Conferring

Once we've modeled, it is time to set the writers free. They're primed creatively and we've "gone first," the way a guide might tackle a tricky rope bridge to show a group of hikers that all will be fine. The best way to help now is to get out of the way and let the students experiment.

But what if they sit and stare at the page? What if they need help? Before helping them with their story, help them as writers. Put the responsibility for thinking and problem-solving directly in their court. Soon, you'll be up and circulating, conferring with kids one on one. But at the beginning of writing time, as I mentioned earlier, facilitators should write, too. Give your writers at least three minutes to work without interruption. That way, when you pull up beside a writer and say, "How's it going?" he or she may have made some progress. Now, the writer may have a question to discuss or some thoughts on applying the day's topic. This, again, is about helping the writers share in the magic, rather than providing all of it for them. Many writers fear what will happen when they slam into a question they can't answer. If we're always there, fixing everything, our students never have to face that fear. If we let them struggle a little in class, and then help them problem solve after they've done all they can, they build self-sufficiency for those times when they're writing at home and we're not there to swoop in and save them.

After this priceless time for individual work, instructors should begin to circulate for short conversations. In chapter seven, we'll look closely at setting up and engaging in these conversations, but here are some basics. The goal while having these conferences—conferring— is to help individualize the instruction for each writer's unique project and skill level. While circulating, we can also raise the overall quality of the class' writing in other ways.

While we move around the room, we might:

CONFER ONE-ON-ONE. Ask individual students, "How's it going?" After working through any questions that arise, identify one strategy a writer might try to build on the strengths already showing up in their work. Our goal is to focus the writer's thinking on a tangible aspect of their writing. This narrow focus gives writers control over their craft. They aren't simply putting words on the page helter-skelter. They're artfully arranging them for a reason. The writer's perspective on her work enlarges. No longer is he simply writing this one story, he's practicing an art form and growing in mastery.

ASSEMBLE A CONFERRING GROUP. Sometimes a quick walk around will make it clear that several writers are struggling with the same question. Invite those students to the carpet area and address the issue together. By conferring in a group, you save precious conferring time and also give peers the opportunity to collaborate, brainstorm, and build on one another's ideas. Eventually, students will learn to problem solve in this way without your help.

PAUSE AND LIFT THE LEVEL. If, while talking to a student or a group, an issue comes up that may help the entire group, call "freeze," and share a quick gem. Use specific, strong passages from the young writer's work, if possible. By highlighting the student's discovery, we make them the expert and we also reinforce what success in our classroom looks like. "Look at this meaningful learning," our subtext says. "This kind of discovery is what we're all aiming for."

☆ LATER ☆

"I'll share later," Yoshi says, shrugging.

Time is running short, but something tells me not to push her. We play Zoom-Mooz. Middle school energy crackles between the boys and girls.

When class ends and everyone else piles out of the classroom, Yoshi hesitates.

"Would you like to read now?" I ask.

"Umm..." she falters. "It's late and..."

"If you have time, I do, too. I'd like to hear what you've written."

So, she starts to read. Her scene is about a tender first kiss. Halfway through, she looks up at me, checking to see if what she's written is okay. Her words are gorgeous and full of emotional depth.

I nod, grateful that I didn't push her to read in front of her peers. When she finishes, I try to put into words what it feels like to witness a writer reading words she wrote from her heart.

"I'm really proud of you," is what comes out. "That is some excellent writing." She lights up the room with her smile.

Sharing

We've established that writing can be difficult. So, why do we do it? We write to explore our thoughts and the landscape of our imaginations...and then to communicate those ideas, images, and beliefs with others. Without sharing, writing is only half done. For this reason, it is important to provide a sharing opportunity each session. Many times, just one sentence is enough. Try a popcorn share where the first reader tosses a ball to the next reader until all have had the chance to play. Or, to cover more ground, writers can share with partners.

Many writers resist sharing. It's risky to put the images that live in our imaginations out for the world to see. Sharing our writing exposes our beliefs, ideas, thoughts, and feelings. Ideally, our classroom is a safe place, one where taking this risk with peers is a perfect first step toward building confidence. Be mindful, though, that dynamics between students or other factors can make risk taking counter productive.

Imagine the little one who stands shoulder-deep in the water, biting his lip, wondering if it's truly safe to try to swim the distance between where he stands and where you wait. "It's okay," you say. "I'm here for you." Often, this is all he needs. He plunges in, and when he makes it into your arms, he bursts into delighted giggles. "I did it, I really did it!" We need to be that cheerleader, opening up opportunities for our students to push themselves, but never insisting or putting them on the spot. Later, we can pull a writer aside and discuss ways to make them feel more comfortable, or figure out why sharing, for them, will not work in this class. While sharing is a highly important element of our writing workshops, we should keep in mind that forced risk taking often leads to disaster.

Depending on your students' skill levels, sharing time is a fantastic opportunity to practice giving feedback. With the youngest writers, having one or two share a compliment is enough. For older writers, adding questions to the mix can help them think critically as they listen. Advanced writers might be shown a model feedback conversation and then sent to work in pairs so they can give and receive more substantial feedback.

Casting a Line

Before finishing your session, leave your writers with a final question, suggested activity,or thinking homework. Lots of obstacles can be bypassed by giving our writers room ahead of time to consider next scenes. Then, choices feel considered rather than forced.

Of course, not all writers will think about their writing between sessions. However, those who would like to and who need the extra time will appreciate the extra notice. I find that when a couple of kids do think things over and come back with well-considered ideas, others take note and begin rising to the challenge, too.

FIRST...

Brainstorm visually—or mind-map—the concept of an opening ritual. What if you had one for your own writing practice? What elements would calm your mind and help you transition into a playful state? What parts of this idea might you use as part of an opening ritual for a class?

AND THEN...

Flip back through this section. Consider: Which parts of the lesson are most likely to feel natural for you? Which will be a stretch? On what element of Writerly Play lessons would you like to focus first as you begin to add play into your teaching practice?

CHAPTER FOUR

the Improvisational Coach

Side-coaching allows facilitators to use the group's energy to shape space for creativity. Through questions, suggestions, and improvised decisions we guide the players into spontaneity and discovery. Side-coaching is used primarily to facilitate games, but it is also a strategy that spills across the rest of the lesson. Before students dive into the games themselves, we'll look at how side-coaching works as a teaching tool.

The magic begins the moment the first student walks through the door.

WEAVING *the* SPELL

Once students experience the power and fun of the games, they can't wait to dive in. As facilitators, our first goal is to create the kind of space that allows for genuine play.

I can't tell you how many times I've wished I could time-travel to the end of the first day with a class, just for a minute. What they need is a vision for what the workshop can be, and once they have this understanding, we're off and running. Unfortunately, sometimes it takes quite a lot of spell weaving to help students catch the vision enough to engage. And if they don't engage, we can't have the collaborative experience of playing together.

Engaging is simply the decision to play. Will they, or won't they? The reasons they might not are many. Maybe they aren't sure their ideas are good enough. Maybe they're not sure what the rules are and they can't stand being wrong. Maybe they're worried someone will laugh at them.

It's a vulnerable place, having the best kinds of fun. When we laugh and goof around, we're

Our first goal is to create a space in which we can all let down our armor and explore.

daring not to worry about looking cool. Anxiety is exacerbated when the facilitator is also concerned about his or her own success. Players are on high alert when they enter this new experience. *We're playing improv games?* they think. *Oh, I'm much too cool for that. Everyone else can look dumb. I'll just keep my cool over here on the sidelines.* Students have supersonic radar for ego. If players catch even a hint of it, they know that when push comes to shove, the facilitator won't take the fall for the group. Someone else will suffer the social humiliation. From that point on, players are armed and ready for battle.

As the class begins, our first objective is to weave a protective spell over the classroom. We're creating a space in which we can all let down our armor and explore. In chapter eight, we will examine how to set up a safe environment for a first-time class, as well as look at a variety of other classroom management strategies. For now, let's focus on the basic pathway to a spellbound classroom. This path must be followed even if this is your fiftieth class with the same players. If we shortcut the process, we risk launching into rocky territory.

In chapter one, we considered why movement is the doorway to play. By moving our bodies, we focus on a simple physical task. Say we start by walking in zigzag lines. Now, at least part of our brain is engaged. We're distracted enough not to notice that we've just been asked to walk in polka dots, and that we're actually hopping from spot to spot in the classroom in a way we'd never have done a moment ago. From polka dots, it's not too far of a leap to walking as though we're hot-footing on sunbaked sand. Or walking as though we feel excited. And then thinking about the things that make us feel excited. And then remembering a specific time we felt excited personally, and striking a pose of ourselves at that moment.

Wait, we think. *I'm grinning my goofy grin and someone might see*. But then, we look around the classroom and realize everyone is grinning. *This class isn't so bad*, we think. *Yeah, this class is kind of awesome, actually.*

Every facilitator manages the pathway to a playful space differently. Some use the same doorway every time, which builds familiarity. Some mix it up, using each fresh invitation to excite the players about the surprises to come. The important thing is never to forget that no matter how experienced the players are, each session must start with movement and basic play. To begin, we don't ask the players to act like anything. First we ask them to move, and when they're in motion, we gauge how quickly we can move into emotive action, which is a bigger risk. Only then should we transition into action that is rooted in their stories, a deeper risk still.

Side-Coaching

We help students move into this risk-taking space by side-coaching. Side-coaching is another name for facilitating the class, using questions, calls and suggestions, and keeping the games flowing. In some ways, side-coaching is a form of narration. But instead of telling a story, we're inviting each player to create a story of his or her own. In many ways, the process is similar to a guided meditation.

At first, side-coaching can feel odd or intrusive. We worry that by injecting our own suggestions and ideas into the space, we're directing the players' stories. We notice that when we speak, players look at us rather than staying engaged in the game. Students are programmed to stop and listen to teachers, so it takes practice for everyone to become comfortable with this new way of working together. At its best, side-coaching becomes a narrative track that provides a life

preserver for players. They can tap into and slip out of the narration, engaging with suggestions as well as following their imaginations when new ideas spark.

Side-coaching can sound like a series of what-if suggestions. Sometimes side-coaching poses a choice or collection of choices. Often the narration is punctuated with the word "notice…" Side-coaching is an art with many layers to it, but it starts with the improv-based practice of saying yes.

Say Yes

Writerly Play grew out of the art of improvisational theatre, so it's probably not surprising that the foundation of our games and activities is the principle of saying yes. When actors first learn to improvise, they begin by learning this skill. The concept is that when a player introduces an idea, instead of rejecting it, the other player must accept the suggestion and add new details to take the scene further. This response is more difficult than one would think. Why is our immediate answer to most suggestions a resounding no? Often, the trouble is that an idea is not what we expected. We can't see where this new direction will lead. We had a plan that our partner's idea completely derails. We're no longer in control. We seize up with fear and shout, "NO!"

In fact, even in brainstorming sessions, you'll hear no hundreds of times. Someone says, "What if we *xxx*," and then someone else interrupts, "No, no, no, what if we *xxx*?" It's a simple, natural reaction. Many times, we think we are brainstorming by replacing someone else's idea with our own. But we're literally saying no. We're dismissing one another's ideas in favor of our own.

Saying yes starts with the facilitator. We say yes by acknowledging the group as they come in, accepting the emotional and physical space they bring into the classroom with them. Yes means starting more slowly or quickly than we intended. Yes invites us to accept our own wacky ideas as they show up while we're facilitating. When we say yes, we build on what happens in the classroom, letting the ideas players introduce affect the direction of our facilitation. This is why we can't script our sessions. We don't know what will happen. Instead, we have to be ready to say yes and build the experience out of the group's energy.

The fact is that no is often simpler. When I'm tired or feeling vulnerable, my funky mood often translates into a session that just doesn't work. When I mentally review, I realize the trouble was a whole lot of no. My no attitude wormed into my facilitation and infected the class. The best-case scenario is that I realize what's happening midstream. Then, I can stop, adjust, and dive back in with a renewed commitment to saying yes.

Helping players build their saying-yes skill is key to the Writerly Play experience, too. A variety of improv games have the sole purpose of developing this skill. Should your class need focused attention in this area, make the primary goal of some of your game playing be the intentional practice of saying yes. The practice will reap huge rewards for your writers within their group work as well as their own writing.

So, how do we begin?

Each new game brings fresh energy to a group. However, introducing new games is also a facilitation challenge. Ideally, at the beginning of a class, we use games that require no explanation at all. We teach them one side call at a time. "Everyone, stand up," we say. "Okay, now, let's move around the empty space, trying not to let any part of the room be empty for too long. Perfect. Yes, be careful not to collide with any furniture, and keep moving. We're moving at a normal speed. Let's call this speed five. What if you moved at a speed six?" and so on. We're

☆ A DISASTER DEMO ☆

I knew I was in for trouble when the students arrived. They were a particularly difficult class, and today, six extra visitors were checking out class for to decide if they'd want to join next term.

I couldn't even get the kids seated in a circle, because two of my enrolled students kept dive tackling each other. One of the other students was also in the mix, and I had no control because I didn't know his name. "Hey you," wasn't going to cut it.

So, I went against my instincts, and before having the students' full attention, I said, "Everybody up, let's start moving around the room."

We moved in swirly lines, in right angles, and in polka dots. I managed to keep anyone from getting hurt, but we never got any further than moving and freezing before the demo students had to leave.

I was sure no one was going to sign up. And, no one did. But I did learn a few things. One: a demo in a class where I struggle to maintain control may not be productive. Two: The games DO work. Even though we didn't have extreme amounts of fun, we did move away from violence. If I'd had more time, I'm sure we would have played more. Three: You can't win every time. Sometimes the best thing to do is accept what can be reasonably done. There's no use in blaming ourselves when the cards are stacked against us. In the end, we didn't have any true disasters. We were all safe. Next time, I may even be able to take myself a little less seriously.

teaching the class how to move and what the boundaries of the game are, and helping the players engage physically.

From here, we might go anywhere. We might move the class into a circle and introduce a new game step by step. We might transition into a movement game to help writers build a character. What we wouldn't want is to stop the momentum to explain a new game in all of its intricate detail. Players want to be right, so if we give them the opportunity, they'll raise their hands and ask a million "But what if…?" questions.

Whenever possible, our goal is to weave the games together so seamlessly that players don't even realize a new game is beginning. Introduce the more complex games later in the session, when momentum isn't as vital. In particular, games with actors and audience members should be saved until a facilitator is sure the students feel safe with one another. Even so, the best way to introduce a new game is to teach it in layers. To begin, call two volunteers to start a scene in simple, physical motion. Once they're engaged, call "freeze" and give the next instruction. Keep progressing until the first players have achieved the basic goals of the game. To further develop the game, call two new volunteers and coach them through the next level of the game. Keep adding challenges as you give the rest of the class opportunities to play, making use of their time as audience members to learn the game.

Calls-Shorthand

One fantastic way to save time and improve focus in the classroom is to teach a basic set of calls. These calls become shorthand that makes facilitation much simpler. You don't have to use a whole sentence when a few words will do.

Some of the most useful calls include:

FREEZE: The most important call of all. When the facilitator calls freeze, players should stop mid-sentence—keeping their bodies still, while also active and engaged—as they listen for the next instruction. Freeze doesn't mean one should drop what he or she is doing and turn to the facilitator. Freeze acts like a magic arctic wind, stopping everyone in their tracks for a second.

GO/MOVE/MELT: Some facilitators use a specific call when they are ready for the players to move again. I find I need different words in various situations, so I usually don't set a specific word. However, for younger groups of students or for classes who need firmer classroom management, setting a word can be useful. One of my favorite tricks with younger groups is to set a ridiculous word, such as hippopotamus. Then, when I'm ready for them to move, I can go through a silly list, such as "Aardvark, Hamburger Helper, Zebra… Hippopotamus!" This strategy keeps the class listening, and transforms what might otherwise feel like heavy-handed class management into an entertaining game.

DOUBLE-TIME: One of the first challenges to overcome when players start for the day is the lazy lean. Draping on desks and slouching in chairs is the opposite of play. When we need an infusion of energy, double-time is often irresistible. In most cases, I call "double-time," and the snarkiest of players will start running around the room. The thing is, a few seconds ago, these players were melting into the wall. Now they are playing a game with me, stretching my boundaries. They're playing and they don't even realize it yet. Next, I call a series of freezes, challenging them to be able to run and stop on a dime, or slo-mo, mixing up the speeds to keep them safe. Soon, they're engaged with the game, and they've forgotten they didn't eat their Cheerios this morning.

SLO-MO: Slo-Mo asks players to treat their bodies as if they were huge rubber bands. We're not lifelessly slogging. We're actively stretching to get to where we're going, just at a very slow speed. Slo-Mo helps players gain physical control over their bodies and helps redirect hyper energy. The more Slo-Mo can be a game the better. Think: what crazy maneuvers can you do without losing control? Slo-Mo requires control, and thus takes practice and modeling to be used to its full benefit.

FULL-BODY WHISPER: This call helps reign in volume. Like Slo-Mo, Full-Body Whisper is not meant to be timid. One must whisper with all of one's might. Thus, whispering becomes a game, rather than a limitation.

PLANE OVERHEAD: Sometimes we need to help our players claim the full power of their own voices. When we're working on projection, using "plane overhead" can make speaking up a game, too.

ONE TO TEN: Depending on the level of control a particular class needs, sometimes using the numbers one through ten to adjust speed or volume can be a helpful tool. I tend to use this call early on in a class as we're learning how to play. Then, I move away from using it as the players find their own rhythm.

Silence and Verbalization

When players are in motion and experimenting with play, one of the next challenges is keeping each player focused on his or her own ideas. While the energy from other players is essential, the funny, entertaining snippets flying around the room are distracting, too. Here's another challenge of play. Most players find it difficult to let go and playfully experiment on their own. It's like trying to do yoga alone in the living room. When others play, one thinks, *I can do that, too!* and takes a risk of his or her own, adding to the creativity and positive momentum in the room. If players are overly focused on their friends, though, they either try to snatch attention or are unable to think their own thoughts.

Maintaining focus is another skill players develop through experience and exposure to the games. Once they understand the power the games have to inspire and shape their stories, they are self-motivated to make the tiny adjustments needed to avoid distraction. As a facilitator builds this awareness and skill level in the classroom, it helps to ask players to "turn off their voices" as a focusing tool. The challenge to move silently and expressively lessens the temptation to interrupt a friend with every brilliant new idea.

Sometimes, asking players to verbalize is also important. When they are in their own space and narrating their experiences, they can focus on their ideas in a way they wouldn't be able to do

Maintaining focus is a skill players develop through experience and exposure to the games.

while thinking silently. For instance, when a player is developing a setting in Build-a-Setting, he or she needs to move deeply into an imagined world. To do so, the player needs to create that verbal lifeline.

It's not as simple as moving from silence to verbalization as players progress. Instead, verbalization is another balance the facilitator manages throughout the workshop. Keep in mind that if sharing is important to your players, you'll want to give the class time at the end of the game to share their best ideas. The payoff of being heard and having one's creativity acknowledged is worth the wait and usually motivates stronger focus throughout the game.

If you have the game Apples to Apples, pull out the deck of cards. If not, take out a stack of index cards and write one noun per card until you have about twelve cards. Then, tell a story out loud, flipping over a card every few sentences. Weave whatever word is on the card into the next part of the story. Practice saying yes to whatever word comes up. Rather than dismissing the word by tossing out a random phrase or by making it into a one-off joke, try hard to include the word in the story itself. Let the word change the direction the story leads next. Practice the flexibility required when you have one idea in mind but must include a completely unexpected element.

Our job is to see what's happening and make the most of it.

A FACILITATOR'S TOOLS

Facilitators are present, aware, ready for any surprise, and bring their best energy to the classroom.

Most of us have watched improv sports, so it's no wonder that we are under the impression that acting is about being the biggest, the funniest, or the one with all the ideas. In point of fact, the most successful actors are the ones who are most present. These actors take in what their fellow players give and make the most of each moment. As they say yes and magnify the humor, energy, and inspiration of everyone on stage, these re-actors shine. For those of us who don't feel like the clever one, or who don't always have the funny comeback line, this is fantastic news. As facilitators, we play this role, too. Our job is to see what's happening in our classroom and make the most of it.

Note the difference between arriving in class with a perfectly scripted story for our warm-up, or starting with a simple prompt and noticing how one student starts pretending to walk a dog. We go with the idea, magnifying the concept until all the players are walking alligators and pterodactyls. Our best facilitation tool is simply to be present, to notice.

Energy and Tempo

Two other key tools are energy and tempo. Nearly every hurdle in class can be overcome with positive momentum. When players are lagging, we turn on our enthusiasm and keep it turned up high until the class has found their rhythm. When players are frenetic and bouncing off the walls, we concentrate our attention to help players move in slo-mo and use full-body whisper until all of that heightened energy is laser-focused on the creative problem of the day. When someone is interrupting the flow, we toss out another suggestion to keep the narration going until the majority of the class is with us and no longer distracted.

Wherever the facilitator focuses her attention, the players turn, too. That's why it's important to be ready to move right past a distraction, or to have a simple way to pull a player out of the game for a moment until he or she is ready to play again. Everything screeches to a halt when you stop playing for a side discussion. Rather than allowing one or two struggling students to take away from everyone's learning, whenever possible, focus on the students who are with you. Particularly for classes that need direction and management, the goal should always be to keep the game going. If the game is in motion, the class will be, too. Your focus on the game will provide the opportunity for struggling students to rise to the occasion. Often, our faith in their ability to join in is all they need to re-engage.

Humor and Surprise

Humor and surprise are the other important tools a facilitator uses. Nothing breaks through armor like making a joke at our own expense. When we're the silliest one in the classroom, we remove the risk that players feel of being humiliated or looking ridiculous. We help everyone save face. Humor can also deflate most conflicts. When students are gearing up for a power struggle, the best way to distract them is with humor.

It's tempting to think that humor requires that we be witty or the Comeback King. Actually, surprise easily adds humor to facilitation. Try tossing a

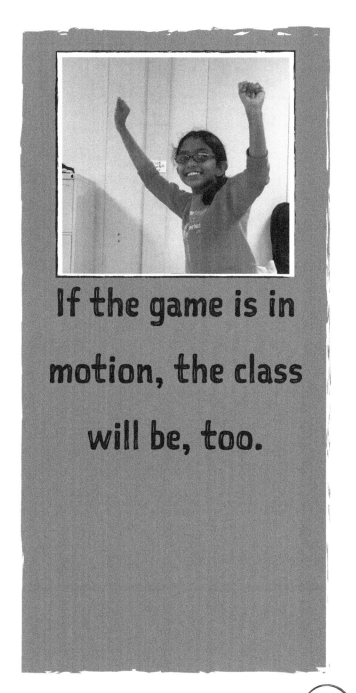

If the game is in motion, the class will be, too.

comment into your side-coaching that no one expects. Give an over-the-top suggestion, such as "How might your character get to school? Walk? Rollerblade? Ride her flying armadillo?"

Surprise inspiration such as the flying armadillo can then become the class joke for the day. The flying armadillo shows up and becomes funnier as she returns repeatedly. By allowing surprise into our facilitation, we show our students what being open to spontaneity looks like. And when students never know what we'll say next, they can't help but listen. Soon, following our example, they begin to let themselves improvise and accept some of their more wacky ideas, too.

→ TRY THIS!

Stretch your absurdist muscles. Allow yourself to free associate out loud or on paper. Start with the phrase "What if..." and play with unexpected combinations: "What if a pancake tornado struck?," "What if we started an elephant roller derby?," and so on. Brainstorm for five minutes and then review what ideas struck you as the funniest. Why were they funny? Tuck any gems away for use when your class needs a laugh to surprise them back into play.

Download a storyboard page from the Writerly Play site and using words and/or images, fill in the boxes to tell the story of a time when someone cheered you on in such a way that it inspired you to push further. Why were you about to give up? What did the person who cheered you do or say that inspired you to keep trying? How did you feel having accomplished something you didn't think you could do at first?

Our facilitation communicates that we believe in our students.

CHEERING FROM *the* SIDELINES

We're the coach who never gives up, the one who believes in our students even when they don't believe in themselves.

Ultimately, our facilitation communicates to the students that we know they are up to the creative challenge we're posing. We are confident they have access to the answers they need. All they must do is answer the question we've posed. If they don't have an idea, that's okay because we've provided a few examples for them to try. We show by example that it's safe to experiment with one idea and then rewind and try something new. The subtext through the entire experience is that we believe in them, we're delighted with their ideas, and we can't wait to see how they'll surprise us (and themselves) next.

Facilitating the Thinking Process

Side-coaching guides reluctant writers from a blank mind into a possibility that can be shaped on the page. For enthusiastic writers, side-coaching slows down the process so skills can be developed further. We often mix grade levels together, and this is because players can learn regardless of how many times they have played the games before. With a new character, a new setting, or a new story concept, suddenly the game is a brand-new creative challenge.

No one would assume that after painting one canvas, he or she knew everything there was to know about painting. Instead, a painter thinks, *Now that I know how to create a sunset, I want to try adding a desert island in the foreground*. Or, *Now I want to try a cityscape.* Or, *Now I want to play with perspective*. The artist wants to develop his or her current skills, try something new, or continue working on a skill not yet achieved. Writing is this same way. We can help our advancing students learn how to identify what they are doing well and how to build on that momentum. Seeds for this development can be planted in the facilitation of the games. As we toss in some challenging questions, those students ready to engage with them think, *Huh. I never thought of that. I wonder...*

Specifics

Games can easily focus the players' attention on the details. As we ask questions and suggest possibilities, we need not shy away from specifics. If we ask, "What do you smell? Roses? Salty-sea air? Rotting bananas?" the likelihood is not that the students will choose one of our ideas. In most

cases, they will choose an answer with the amount of specificity that we've presented. *Of course they don't smell rotting bananas*, they think. *Actually, they're at the beach next to an ice cream stand and they smell vanilla ice cream and baking waffle cones.* If we ask, "What do you smell? Flowers? Something in the air? Fruit?" in most cases, they'll just choose one of our options and never take it further. Our suggestions don't pose a dissonance with their idea. *Obviously they smell flowers—they're outside.*

Physically moving through a scene also helps players overcome the tendency to wind up for a scene as they write. They don't have to write out every single detail about their character, exhausting themselves before they even get to the part of their story they want to write. They've played through all those details and have thought of a way to shape them into an interesting scene. Also, playing through a scene makes showing rather than telling simple. We can't act *feeling frustrated* for very long. One can only flop into a chair so many times. *Ah*, we think. *Maybe I should bake cookies while I'm frustrated. Then, I can slam the bowl on the counter. I can crush the eggs and then dig the shells out of the batter. I can hurl them shard by egg-shard into the sink.* Now, *frustrated* is tangible.

→ THREE-MINUTE BRAIN-STRETCH

Think of three games you know well. On a blank piece of paper with colored pencils or pens, diagram how you might make those three games flow together. Which game would start the sequence? Where would players stand or sit? Then, how would they play? At what point would you transition to the next game? How would the shape of the game shift? How would you bring the game to a close?

When playing, the answer to nearly every question is yes.

SHAPING *the* EXPERIENCE

The goal is to make the session one complete experience that flows from beginning to end.

Since we don't want to stop the flow of the games to answer questions, our first approach to teaching new games is to try to demonstrate as we play. However, sometimes questions are inevitable. At some point early in a class, it's good to set up a few ground rules about questions.

The first helpful guideline is that players should try to answer their own questions. If a player is unsure whether their idea fits the game, they should just try it. If their attempt doesn't work, and their idea throws the game off course, the facilitator can always call freeze and redirect the group. If the question is related to a specific detail in a writer's story, that writer can discuss and clarify his or her thinking with the facilitator during writing time.

Another important point to address early on is that the answer to most questions is yes. Most questions are rooted in the fear of doing something wrong. As players start to learn that the games leave room for choices, this concern subsides.

In order to create an environment where questions don't interrupt the flow, it's important to avoid pitfalls and ways that players might become confused. Often games do have rules. When someone makes a mistake, they end up in the middle or out of the game for a round. The rules provide the structure for the game and are part of the fun. When playing competitive games, I usually introduce the rules without anyone facing consequences at first. We play, practicing for a bit until we're all clear on how the game is played. Then, we agree it's time to play for real. Competition can be more or less poisonous depending on group dynamics. Most times, particularly if the consequences are no big deal—being out for a few seconds until the next round, or being the next person in the middle—mild competition makes the game more fun. It's important to make sure never to enforce a rule that someone didn't know, though, if we don't want to end up in an endless cycle of "what if this happens" questions every time a new game is introduced.

TRANSITIONS

Side-coaching takes the group through each game, but side-coaching is actually the foundation of the entire class. We coach the players from the invitation into the connection, into the games, into the modeling, and so on. In each transition, we step into our side-coaching role.

Some transitional phrases that work well include:

- Let's all stand up.

- Find a space in the room where you haven't stood yet today.

- Shake that character off and move somewhere new. Five-four-three-two-one…

- Can we make a circle in five counts? Five-four-three-two-one…

- Freeze. Make your body into the shape of a cupcake (or some other silly shape).

- Freeze. Make a monster face. Make a lemon face.

- Freeze. Put your body into a neutral position, hands by your sides, feet under your shoulders.

- Freeze. Turn so you can't see anyone's eyes.

- Freeze. Close your eyes.

- Take ten seconds to describe whatever you haven't had time to describe. Double-time!

- Freeze. Show me with your fingers how many more minutes you need to finish this worksheet.

- We're going to come to a circle in two minutes. Challenge yourself. Can you put three more sentences on the page?

- Okay, you have thirty seconds, finish up that sentence.

- Freeze. You'll have more time to write, but I want to tell you about what Mandy and I noticed just now. (Then we share a quick insight into the writing process.)

- Freeze. A lot of us are confused about… Does anyone have any suggestions? (OR What this question's asking is…)

Stop and Adjust

Sometimes it isn't possible to redirect the class through side-coaching. In these cases, I call students to a circle and we problem solve as a group. The conversation is basically an assessment of what we feel isn't working and what we can do together to make the games work better. This kind of conversation works much more effectively if the class is invested in the games working because they have experienced the fun of them already. If they have not, sometimes after a quick discussion of what's not working, I cast a vision for why we're playing and provide a picture of the possibilities. Then, we might play a more controlled game with the focus of finding our rhythm.

Side-coaching is what makes a Writerly Play lesson a magical experience. Players may not be able to put their fingers on exactly why they were inspired, but they can't wait to come back the next session and have the experience again. Whether we side-coach in a small way for a one-on-one lesson or to facilitate an entire lesson in a larger group setting, this strategy is an essential part of shaping a creative space for our students.

TRY THIS...

Think of an activity with which you are familiar but which is reasonably challenging. Grocery shopping is a good example. Imagine yourself as the player and also as the side-coach. Script a side-coaching narrative to help guide your imagined self through the trip. Have fun with it, and don't forget to let yourself be surprised.

AND THEN...

Practice your habit of writing regularly by reflecting on the following questions in your journal. When have you used side-coaching or something like it previously? What strengths do you bring to your side-coaching? Are you thorough? Funny? Spontaneous? A great listener? Where might you play to your strengths with side-coaching?

the Give and Take of Games

When we think of a game, we often think of a stand-alone activity along the lines of tag or capture the flag. In Writerly Play lessons, the games are more fluid and adaptable. Games are the foundation of the classroom management, the instruction, and the application of skills. In order to improvise with games, we need to understand their basic structures and how those structures work to shape class dynamics.

→ ONE-MINUTE BRAIN-STRETCH

Picture the worst possible classroom dynamic you can imagine. What's happening with the students? What is the mix of personalities? Then, make it worse. Add a fire drill or an argument on the playground just before class. Make it even worse, one more time. Maybe it's a day when you're being observed by an administrator. Notice how your body feels right now, while you're thinking of that situation. Then, think of one thing that could happen in the middle of your horrible scenario to make you and your class laugh. The wilder the idea, the better. Now, notice how you feel. Take your laughter with you into the next chapter.

What kind of energy do your writers need to explore the day's concept?

READING the WRITERS

Before launching an instructional game, identify your students' mood, focus, and energy level. Once you know the place from which the class is starting, you can help them transition into a state of play.

Consider the writers' current state. Are they droopy? Reserved? Frustrated? Scattered? Hyper? Taking all of these factors into account, make a quick decision and launch the class. The flow of games will depend on your classroom management and teaching objectives. What kind of energy do your writers need in order to explore the day's concept? What sequence of games will best achieve this energy? Approach this challenge playfully and you'll model an openness to inspiration. Your attitude will do more than any words could to help your students dare to open themselves, as well.

Before we focus on the specifics of any one game, let's start by thinking big picture about the flow we're aiming to create. If, as you read, you'd like to refer to specific games, see the detailed descriptions in appendix one.

For example, say your class comes in after being cooped up all day for rainy-day recess. They're bouncing off the walls, unable to keep their hands off one another, and irritable to boot. You had planned to play Scene Tag to introduce the idea of dialogue, but you're afraid the minute you start moving the class around the room, they'll seize the opportunity for full-body tackles. On top of that, you know you can't sit them down in a circle and talk to them because if you do, someone might just jump out of their skin.

So, approaching the challenge playfully, you might appoint a tape captain and assistant, and ask them to make masking tape X's spread around the classroom, one for each player. While they are busy doing this, you help the rest of the class corral their bags and materials in a corner of the room. Then, you ask each player to go stand on an X. To begin, and to make sure you have everyone's attention, you might start with a hybrid version of Slideshow. In this game, on his or her X, each player poses in the shape of an item you suggest. Use humor to capture the students' attention, and a short time limit to keep them on their toes. For instance, "Make your body into the shape of a mushroom, 5...4...3...2...1. Now make your body into the shape of a giraffe, 5...4...3...2...1," and so on. If you feel players need even more movement, ask them to do three jumping jacks between poses or to shake off each pose for a certain number of counts. When you have more focused attention from them, consider having the students switch x's between poses. Or ask them to pair up with one other player at an X and pose together.

Now that they're in partner teams, you can give the players scene poses to make, such as "You're trying to wrap a golf club for your dad" or "You're decorating your classroom for the Halloween party." Once they're able to freeze in these moments without losing focus, raise

☆ BUT... ☆

Every time he enters the room, I tense. I know it is only a matter of time before one of my least favorite words comes out of his mouth.

"Let's make a circle. First, toss your name across the–"

"BUT," he interrupts, earlier even than expected. "You can't throw your name. That's impossible."

"Let's imagine that our names are the shape of a ball and we can toss them across the circle," I say, trying not to grimace.

"Rebecca," the smallest girl in our group says, tossing her name as though it is feather-light.

"BUT it's a name, not a thing," he insists, refusing to catch her name.

"We're..." I catch myself. My voice is already rising. I stop and breathe. Then, thankfully, I have an idea.

"Let's vote. We can play one of two games. In one, we'll pretend our names can be tossed across the circle like a ball. In the other, we'll pass Zoom around the circle one way, like this, and Mooz the opposite way. Everyone is allowed to switch the direction we're passing twice. We'll see how fast we can pass the words from one person to another without accidentally sending the wrong word the wrong way."

We vote, and it turns out the whole group prefers Zoom-Mooz. After the vote, probably because he knows the group truly wants to play this game, he manages not to interrupt again. Until we move on to the next game: Walk as If.

I'm reminded that every time he says, "BUT..." he looks to his peers for a reaction. Even when they groan, he has turned the entire group's focus to himself. As we continue playing, I consider how else I may help this student work with the class rather than hijack the group. At least, I've figured out one strategy that works, and as long as I continue to experiment, I know I'll find others. Also, I've taken the very important step of settling down my own frustration. I've stuck to my strategy of using games to keep the flow of the class going. The mood in the classroom is playful and proactive rather than blocked. Over time, I'm confident that even this protesting player will come around and realize he'd rather play and create than dwell on obstacles.

the stakes by giving them a moment or two to speak to one another. Now, you've made it to your original objective: discussing dialogue. To provide instruction about using dialogue in their stories, freeze the group and use the spotlight technique to feature a few of the player teams. As they perform, use side-coaching to encourage interesting dialogue.

Next, move the players back to their own X's and ask them to pose as one of their own characters.

In this pose, prompt them to think of an interesting line of dialogue. Then, ask them to pose as another character in the scene. What might that character say? Through the entire sequence, you're reading the group and considering whether they are ready to move on or whether you need to slow down the progression. Ideally, the point is to make the game so lively and fun that students don't want to horse around because they'd rather play. If the majority of the class is with you, but you have one or two kids who can't make it work, consider sending those couple outliers to audience chairs. Nine times out of ten, the audience will see how much fun everyone else is having and be motivated to join back in.

The sequence may start in an entirely different way if your class comes in with low energy and droopy attitudes. In this case, you might try a high-energy circle game, increasing the intensity with each prompt until you've got them moving full-speed. Then, you can transition into a movement game that moves kids into partner pairs, where the entire class can simultaneously play out scenes. Side-coach to provide the instruction about dialogue. Then, when your students are ready, either move them to a circle and ask each to set a writing goal for the day, or send them off to work right away and circulate to check in about their plans.

Creating a Flow

Used well, the games weave a spell over the classroom. Some days, this magic is easier to achieve than others. However, the basics are always the same. The facilitator must approach the lesson as a playful challenge. The games are the tools with which facilitators help the writers shift into a creative mode, the tools with which they will teach, mentor and guide, and the tools with which they direct the writer's attention to the next steps of his or her project. Ideally, when the writers sit down to write, every distraction is left behind and they have advanced their thinking about their stories. Now they have inspiration and new strategies to push ahead in their work. Games can help in conferring moments, too, allowing writers to move past blocks or consider options without feeling criticized or cornered.

It is tempting to think of each game as a unique entity with its own beginning, middle, and end. We have grown up thinking of games this way. First, we play tag. Then, we're bored so we move on to hide-and-seek. In order to create a flow in a Writerly Play lesson, one must blur all of the boundaries, allowing one game to flow into the next. We can't be afraid to play a movement game in a circle or an improv game using frozen poses, based on the needs of the students in the moment.

What we need to know is:

1. What is my teaching objective?
2. What can the students handle today?
3. Working within those limitations, where should I start, and where should I aim to take the class?

Then, along the way, we make adjustments as needed.

Keep in mind that learning to teach through play is an art. These strategies are not learned in a day, but the results are definitely worth the effort. As you play with the games and your facilitation skills, you encourage your students to play, too. You're modeling the process of experimentation and growth—exactly the risks you're asking of your students. Think of it as a grand game of showing rather than telling, so go easy on yourself and set realistic expectations as you begin. One step at a time, and soon you'll find that magic has sparked in your classroom, too.

A note on classroom management: As you explore the basic game structures on the next pages, you'll see that the games are the core of your classroom management in Writerly Play. Instead of putting regulations in place, aim to enchant the class into learning. However, classroom management is a vital part of successful game facilitation. Chapter eight is dedicated to an exploration of various classroom management strategies, both within games and outside them.

☆ INTERVIEW IN *the* ROUND ☆

"Can't we just write?" one student whines in response to my announcement of our game: Interview.

I know they're craving writing time, but I also know they've been wandering through their stories with rather shapeless ideas and little to no character motivation or forward momentum.

"Circle up," I say, and they come grumbling to the circle. "I know you want lots of writing time, and I promise to give you lots of time after our game. I want to make sure we're all warmed up and ready, though."

We go through a quick round of Eight-Count Shakedown, and as I knew it would, the game leads to laughter. Then, I pull out my imaginary microphone and start asking questions rapid-fire, alternating between serious questions and silly ones, giving a few kids a chance to answer each question as their main characters, keeping the pace quick.

"Okay, one last question," I say, after we've played for about seven minutes. "After you answer, you may head to your writing space. In this next scene, what are you willing to do to get what you want?"

One by one they answer, and then head off to write, and not only are they motivated to write, but the scenes are alive with action and energy.

On a range of 1 to 10, what is your comfort level with teaching through games? What excites you about the possibility? What challenges do you anticipate? Before you read on, think of three games with which you are very comfortable that might be fallback games for you in difficult moments. Mine are Boom-Chica-Boom (not exactly a game), Simon Says, and Choices.

Circle games offer the benefit of eye contact and collaboration.

the BASIC GAME STRUCTURES

The games have varying levels of difficulty, freedom, and control, and can be blended or adapted based on what a class needs on any given day.

Before becoming too focused on the details of any one game, consider how each game works at its core. A game might be about visualizing a setting or stepping into the shoes of a character. The goal, then, isn't to play Character Layer in the exact format it is usually played, but rather to help your students step into the shoes of their characters in whatever way they can on this particular day. Part of strong facilitation involves adapting the games from one shape to another. The flow of one game to another, and the transition of one game shape to another, should be fluid and flexible.

Circle Games

Circle games are often the first games of a lesson. However, these games can be used throughout

Movement games allow players to be in their own space, thinking and creating on their own.

a lesson as well. Bringing the students into a circle and playing a game helps focus attention and move everyone onto the same page. Circle games also offer the benefit of eye contact and collaboration. Energy builds as the players give and take with one another. Strong players model for those who may not know the game and because all players can see one another, learning to play becomes simple.

Most circle games need not be explained prior to playing. Ideally, facilitators teach these games in layers while playing. One need not have a focused class before playing. Playing a circle game can be the focusing tool in itself, making these games an essential resource in the facilitator's toolkit.

Movement Games

During movement games, students use the full range of the classroom. The goal is for players to be in their own space, visualizing and creating on their own. This individual creation is spurred on by the facilitator's side-coaching. All students in the room play at the same time, making these games efficient instructional tools. At first, players may be tempted to perform for or with one another. Part of teaching a class to play movement games well is building their ability not to interrupt one another. Thus, one goal of early play is to help students build concentration and body and voice control.

As with circle games, most movement games can be taught while playing with minimal setup. However, since the facilitator has less control during movement games, it is important to establish boundaries prior to play and any cue words needed such as "freeze." Also, players must have a level of self-control before beginning a movement game. Often the flow is from a circle game directly into a movement game. Movement games offer the most independent thinking and privacy of all the games, and therefore work well for planning, idea generation, and exploration.

Quick-Thinking Games

Quick-thinking games take advantage of the spontaneous reaction that occurs when a group of players are truly in a state of play. In many cases, these games follow a movement game so that players are ready with open minds. With quick-thinking games, we're building the skill of making a choice, trying it out, and then changing the decision later as need be. The ultimate goal is that when students sit down to write, they have the ability to try a possibility and see where it takes them, rather than staring at the blank page for fifteen minutes trying to make the perfect decision.

Quick-thinking games help players generate ideas and can also make excellent warm-up games. These games have the ability to easily introduce the fun of playing games to a new group of

Quick-thinking games help players generate ideas and are always excellent as warm-ups.

players. Since they don't require acting of any kind, these games are safe and simple for even the most reticent of players.

Quick-thinking games shouldn't require a lot of up-front explaining, but may need a quick introduction. They can be played in a circle, but can also be played with a movement component—a fun hybrid option. Particularly when played in a circle, quick-thinking games can shift the dynamic of the class energy. When writers are bored, stuck, frustrated, droopy, grumpy, or argumentative, try throwing in a quick-thinking game with a dash of humor. When the group is simply having a hard time getting started, or clowning around, often playing a quick-thinking game is a more effective behavior solution than a sit-down group problem-solving session.

Tableau Games

The word *tableau*, pronounced "tab-low" is of French origin. Literally, it translates as "picture."

In improv, tableau games highlight frozen moments. While acting out a scene will help a writer understand moment-to-moment flow, tableau games pull the writers above their stories and ask them to choose the most important moments. Thus, tableau games allow high-level thinking. Using a tableau to plan the beginning of a story, for instance, helps young writers move past the minutia of waking up and getting dressed into the essential action. A tableau game can help students to find the perfect right starting moment. Then, when they sit down at the page, they are able to quickly move past the exposition, which may otherwise bore them and use up all their writing energy, and get straight to the "good stuff."

Tableau games provide opportunities for high-level thinking.

Tableau games can be played individually or in groups. Group tableaus help players build on one another's ideas physically. Asking players to create tableaus nonverbally, without preplanning or discussion, adds spontaneity and heightened collaboration. While players might want to know who will be the wolf and who will be Goldilocks, if they build the tableau one player at a time, making instant on-the-spot decisions, they don't have to argue about who will play which role for that split second. The next time around, a new player can try the role of Goldilocks.

Using an audience when playing tableau games offers the added opportunity for audience feedback. This feedback provides important discoveries for the players and for the audience. The audience might notice something about how stories work while they watch the sequence of tableaus, or they might suggest a solution that involves a physical change in the tableau that will make the underlying story work more clearly. These insights often lead to a quick discussion of how a similar concept might apply to the students' stories. Try questions such as "What do we notice about…" or "How might we add conflict (or suspense or characterization or foreshadowing) to this moment?"

Because tableaus are fast paced, they work well when you'd like students to try a number of options. Tableau games usually require more structured setup but can be taught in layers to minimize instruction time. One group models the basics of the game, and each subsequent group adds a layer of complexity, so that by the last group's turn, you can take the game to the desired level of discussion.

Scene Games

Scene games require a certain amount of acting skill, and therefore do not work with every class. Consider age level and focus when determining whether scene games are the best choice for a particular group. When possible, scene games are an exceptional teaching tool. Scene games use the basics of story—character, setting and plot—and are doorways to address nearly every aspect of storytelling. For instance, one might introduce character motivation or a complication rising to a climax through a scene game. Keep in mind that poor improvisation skills will detract from the learning. If you plan to use improvisation games as a larger part of class instruction, invest time in helping the players build their basic acting skills, such as saying yes, using their voices and bodies to convey emotion, staying in character, and building on the scene rather than clowning for the immediate laugh.

Scene games do not always have to be improvised. A facilitator might ask players to act out a simple script or a page of text from a story in order to explore a concept. In this case, students might be learning about subtext (and what an author must explain by adding description) or active scenes (if a page of text offers too much or too little opportunity to move). A scene game can also be narrated by the facilitator so that the players don't have to read. Then, the focus is on putting the story into motion and learning through physicalizing the text.

A note on scene games: Because these games require true collaboration, it is important not to

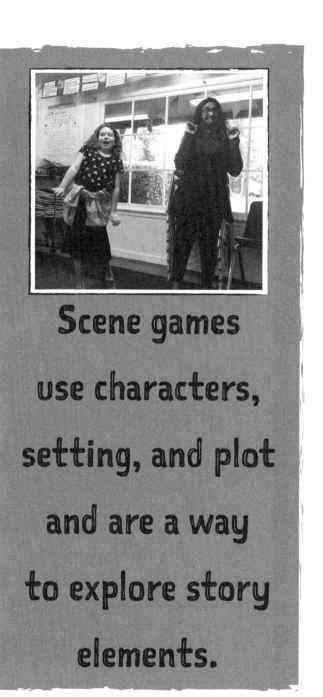

Scene games use characters, setting, and plot and are a way to explore story elements.

use a specific player's story as the scenario for the scene game. For instance, you wouldn't want to put a player on stage as the main character of his own story and have him improvise the next part of the plot with his fellow actors. It is nearly impossible to improvise well—a collaborative process—when authors are frustrated because their own story isn't going the way they wish. Even though the game can be set up as what "might" happen next in a story, feelings can easily be hurt, or plots can be thrown off track with all of the group's suggestions.

Scene games are usually taught by modeling. Ideally, a few players know the game and can model it for the other players. If this isn't the case, the facilitator explains the rules and demonstrates the game with a few players, pausing when additional instruction is needed to clear up details.

In most cases, facilitators break the class into groups of four or five players (more per group makes collaborating on the spot difficult) and with each new scene, a new challenge is added to the game, as in the teaching of tableau games. In this way, the audience is also involved while the game is being played. Scene games need not play out to their bitter end, and in fact work better if they do not. Keep the pace lively by calling *scene* after a minute and a half or two and then calling up a new group of players.

In-the-Moment Games

While scene games usually involve improvisation, for the purposes of Writerly Play, we make a distinction between the more complex scene games and more simple improvisation games. Let's call these games "In-the-Moment" games. They are more casual than scene games. Usually, they involve only one or two players and, depending on the setup, in-the-moment games can be used to build the next part of a story. Often in-the-moment games are played with the entire class spread around the room working in unison. Due to this structure, these games should only be played when the class has a high degree of focus.

In-the-Moment games often lead to on-the-spot discoveries.

In-the-moment games help players make on-the-spot discoveries about their characters and settings, and about events that might further their stories. In-the-moment games can also be used between two players to build skills, particularly by using dialogue in a variety of ways. With some groups, in-the-moment games help give an author a new perspective on his or her story. In these cases, an author might provide a brief description of two characters and a scenario, giving the actors a chance to put their own creativity into the moment. While the author may not ultimately decide that his or her character behaves this way, or to include a similar scene in the story, the outside perspective on the characters sometimes brings the characters to life in a new way.

Another way to improvise casually with a story is for each author to choose a scenario that might happen in a character's life but which won't be included in the story. For instance, a character might get called to the principal's office for breaking a rule, and the author plays the main character. The scene offers the author the opportunity to spontaneously discover how the character reacts when he or she is in trouble. The other player can interpret the principal (who never enters the pages of the actual story) however he or she wishes.

In-the-moment games are usually taught through modeling. Keep the demonstration short and, as in scene games, answer the what-if questions as they arise in play. In many cases, you'll want to pair up or group players up to play simultaneously to use time most effectively.

Since performance and group feedback aren't typically part of in-the-moment games, consider raising the level of play by using the Spotlight tool. At some point during the game, call "freeze." Then, with rapid-fire energy, point to one group and call "spotlight!" Give the group a few moments to play while the rest of the class watches and then spotlight another group. As you transition, highlight what worked well in the game to help raise the level of play and writerly thinking.

Storytelling Games

Storytelling games allow writers to tell their stories aloud in the words they might use later on the page. For groups of young writers who partner well, these games are an excellent way to move past the rough-rough draft and into a more polished idea before putting words on the page. Since most young writers resist the idea of changing anything after it has been put onto the page, using storytelling games first is a great option. Storytelling becomes the first draft, and sometimes the second and third drafts as well. Writing out loud first helps writers stay flexible and willing to revise—if not on the page, at least in their thinking. The facilitator can ask the writers to tell the story, then to rewind, add an element, and tell it again. The partner can ask helpful questions; and most importantly, the young writer hears the story out loud and often finds places where characters, settings, or events need more description or elaboration. In order to set up a storytelling game, move the players around the room and ask them to pair up pinkie-to-pinkie and then toe-to-toe and then elbow-to-elbow. After a few of these challenges, players start pairing with the next possible person and move past sticking

Storytelling games give writers the chance to create a first draft out loud.

with their best friends. When the class is paired well, ask them to face their partner in order to play. For more focus, ask the pairs to sit, which keeps them from wandering around the room. When partners stand for storytelling games, the telling is usually infused with more energy. Model the game and then set the players loose. Remember to establish a basic amount of time players have to complete their telling, and to give them a warning when the limit is approaching. For instance, "Ten more seconds: 10, 9, 8..." For large or rowdy groups, you may need a noisemaker to call their attention back.

Interview Games

Interview games allow facilitators to help players make discoveries through specific questions. With older classes, students might interview one another in pairs, but in general, an interview game works best when hosted by the facilitator. Usually, an interview will take place at the front of the class with four to five players while the rest of the group acts as audience. Interviewing several students at once offers the facilitator the opportunity to pause one writer, move on to another, and return later. The benefit of this strategy is that the pace of the game speeds, pushing players to answer more quickly, while also giving them time to think rather than putting them on the spot.

Interview games use focused questions to help writers make discoveries.

Also, the facilitator can easily switch gears politely if one answer goes on too long.

Interview games usually don't need a lot of explaining and should be intuitive. If you need to explain anything at all, do it quickly and then start the game up as quickly as possible. Often a line of chairs at the front of the room helps establish the space, making for a more official interview feel. Use an imaginary microphone (either an invisible one or a pencil or whatever else is on hand). The microphone heightens the game and makes it feel more theatrical, and thus more energetic and fun.

The Play's the Thing

Part of the fun of facilitating a Writerly Play lesson is making discoveries on the spot. The more we experiment and play with the games, the more alive and energetic our sessions feel. Every Writerly Play lesson plan includes suggested games, but keep in mind that any game is fair play as long as it achieves your objective. Rather than scripting out your games, make sure you know your specific goals. These goals serve as steppingstones to mark your way through class. Then, in the moment, stay open to when a game might help transition the class from one mode to the next, or provide a fun reward for hard work. The larger your toolkit of games, the more flexibility you'll have in the moment. Improvise with your students, and you'll find you can manage nearly all situations that arise with a new game.

TRY THIS...

Think of a task you do with at least one other person that involves some level of problem solving. Two possibilities include cooking dinner or getting ready in the morning. Orchestrate a sequence of made-up games that might move you through the process in an energetic and amusing way.

AND THEN...

Practice your habit of writing regularly by reflecting on the following questions in your journal. What were your favorite games as a child? Do you play any games now? What makes a game fun to you? What elements make an activity feel like a game rather than a task?

Thinking
Out Loud

———————◆———————

Most of what happens when we write is invisible, connection
by connection, inside our minds. For this reason, it's easy to be
tricked into thinking that some people are writers and others
are not. When we, as facilitators, put our thinking into words, we
illuminate the writing process for our students and give them a
trail map to build their skills.

Draw the outline of two human figures (a circle will work, too, in a pinch). In one, list all the ways in which you are a mentor. You might use one word "math," for instance, the name of someone you mentor, or a phrase that reminds you of one mentorship role you play, such as "dance captain." Inside the other outline, list all the ways in which you are currently being mentored. Think about how you're advised by those older than you, by your peers, and also, wonderfully, by those who are younger than you.

A mentor teaches by example, pulling alongside his or her charge.

the MENTORING RELATIONSHIP

Mentors share their stories, provide feedback, and most importantly, believe and invest in their charges' success. Whether we're teaching one-on-one or guiding a full classroom, our role is one of mentorship.

When you think of a teacher-student relationship, what do you picture? What is the teacher's role? And the student's role? Now, consider a mentorship. What does a mentorship look like? How might a mentor go about sharing his or her expertise?

To my mind, a mentor teaches by example, pulling up alongside his or her charge. Mentors actively engage in the craft they're sharing, and when they work with their mentees, in part, they share the story of their own experience. A mentorship is an ongoing relationship. Many mentors engage in mentorship because they know that through reflection and conversation with their charges, they will continue to grow themselves.

I believe that to teach the art of writing, one must take on the role of mentor. It simply doesn't work to approach the teaching relationship as a transaction through which we pass information on to students. To begin, our students will see through us. Writing is a lifelong learning process. Ask any novelist, best-selling or otherwise. When one opens a new document and starts on page one of a new project, no matter how many stories we've written, we are all in the exact same space—at the beginning. We may have a lifetime of experience and comfort with the tools at hand, but we still have to learn each new writing project, discovering the process that works in each new landscape.

What a gift! Our continual learning cycle puts us directly in touch with the emotions and questions our students are facing. We can share the strategies that have worked best for us; our current questions; and perhaps most helpful of all, the story of our mistakes, discoveries, and successes. Remember what we're aiming for? Perspective, play, and practical strategies. We're collaborating to develop real-world solutions with our students, for this particular project, in this particular situation.

Modeling is how we can bring our expertise to the discussion. We aren't bringing our perfection; rather, we're opening up our thinking process and sharing how we weigh options, the strategies we might try in a given situation, and the ultimate decisions we make to end up with words on the page.

Bridging from Play to Practical Strategies

No one doubts the fun of play, or questions the enthusiasm buzzing around a classroom after a game session. What is less clear is how to focus that creative energy onto the page. Think of the energy as a wild forest through which a student wanders until he or she can find the bridge to the hidden castle. Even though the forest is teeming with life, which is great and full of possibility, it is still difficult to find one's way without becoming distracted.

Focusing that creative energy is not impossible, though. What it takes is concentration. We have to find the path and follow it, one step after another. We can admire what's to our right and left, but we can't wander too far off course. Modeling helps students find that path.

Say, for instance, we've just played Slideshow. We've explored various beginnings for our story and have a storm of possibilities in our minds. Now, we must sort through the ideas and make decisions. If we were to model how we'd approach this process, it might look like this:

1. List our ideas.
2. Circle our three favorites.
3. Try each one out aloud for a paragraph or two.
4. Think out loud about why one might work better than the others.
5. Make a last-minute decision to add our favorite part of a discarded idea to our final choice, making a hybrid idea.

Using Your Own Writing

Revision becomes more appreciated with perspective. The reality is that new writers resist revision in a way experienced writers do not. After seeing how much our writing benefits from revision, we forget what it felt like to fear changing our work. Think back. Try to remember the sheer terror you felt at the suggestion of revision. After all the time you'd invested in a story, you'd look back and see all the weaknesses in your work. You likely wouldn't have the slightest idea how to fix the issues, or worse, you wouldn't know what was wrong but still felt that something wasn't right.

Since revision is another part of writing we need to model, one path of least resistance is to invite the class to revise *our* writing rather than theirs. In this nonthreatening way, they begin to experience the fun of playing with words, of seeing what one is trying to say but not quite saying, or how to magnify a stylistic effect. They see how to take out clutter to make the beautiful parts of a scene stand out. They learn to make the dialogue pop and crackle rather than lay limp on the page. After seeing how much can be done, you never know—they may just try it with their own work.

Think back to one of your most challenging revision experiences. Download one of the storyboarding pages at www.writerlyplay.com and storyboard the memory. In each box, either draw an image or list words that represent the major positive and negative turns in the experience. Look over your storyboard and consider how this memory might be used while talking to your charges.

☆ AHA! ☆

"I brought a draft of my first scene to work on with you. This story is written in third person and it feels a little distant. Let's read."

After we finish, she says, "I think it's really good! I have no idea what I'd change."

"Let's take a closer look. I noticed when I read that there were a lot of filter words. That's something I do a lot when I draft. I write, 'she saw,' or 'she felt,' or 'she heard.' But what if I took out 'she said' and instead wrote, 'Red clouds scudded across the sky'?"

Her face lights up. "It's like I'm seeing the clouds, not watching her see the clouds."

I can't help but grin. She's exactly right. "And seeing the clouds makes you feel more in the scene, doesn't it?"

"Yeah! And you do it here, too. Could we take out 'she heard,' and put 'The wind howled'?'"

"Sure, that's an excellent suggestion."

After we find a few other filters, she turns to her own writing. "I wonder if I do this, too. In my story? Can we look?"

"Let's do it!"

Soon, we're finding filters in her writing, too. Our revision process feels like a treasure hunt, not a chore. Not for the first time, I'm thankful for my own imperfections. What fortune that my first-draft writing comes out in need of many different kinds of revision, providing multiple doorways for fantastic learning opportunities.

→ THREE-MINUTE BRAIN-STRETCH

Stand up. In an open space, bend forward and breathe deeply, letting your hands reach toward or brush against the floor. Think of a specific emotional moment in your story. Once you have the moment in mind, slowly roll your way back up to standing—one vertebrae at a time—and when you finally lift your head, let your body transform into the shape of your character's body at the moment you just pictured. How is he standing? Or sitting? Where is she? What is she doing? Try a couple actions that might fit this moment. Your character may have an object in hand. For now, use an imagined one. After you have explored this moment fully, drop forward again and try physicalizing one more emotional moment.

By modeling, we transform the energy generated by the games into actionable ideas.

BUILDING STUDENT CONFIDENCE

During our modeling time, we help students realize what they already know, and provide practical examples of how to apply and build on that knowledge.

Practical strategies start with modeling. What have the students tried before that worked well? What might they try now? By modeling, we help transform the creative energy generated by the games into actionable ideas.

When I model, my goal is to send students to their desks with one specific focus to consider as they write. Of course, there are many elements they'll deal with in any given scene, but if they have a strategy for working on the dialogue in their scene, they can finish the writing session with success. They can say, "I wanted my characters to speak in short sentences that sounded like real people talking over one another... and I did it!"

A variety of focuses you may want to consider for modeling and conferring are listed in appendix two.

Thinking/Application Time

One way to make sure your students are ready to write is to give them a chance to apply the skill right away. After modeling a strategy on the board, ask the students to try it themselves right where they're sitting. They might try the strategy in their notebooks or out loud with a partner. It's one thing to feel as though one knows how to do something when someone else is doing it, and another completely when one tries it out himself.

With the youngest of students, applying a strategy may be the simple act of making a decision about a character's favorite color or animal. By doing so, the writer is differentiating this character as a unique person with his or her own personality. Then, the facilitator may model a few options for how this character's favorite color could show up in the story. While the ways our youngest writers tuck information into a story won't be as complex as those of our more advanced writers, the process of hearing a concept, thinking about how it applies to one's own character and/or story, and then applying it in writing is the same. By beginning to practice this process with the simplest of concepts, we prepare our students to continue to use the process as their writing becomes more complex.

Once students have wrestled the question or strategy in their own work, ask them a few questions. Successes and struggles during the few moments of application turn into teaching tools. After students have expanded their thinking and heard additional perspective from their peers, they are ready to go work on their own.

Redirecting "Copying"

Copying peers is an issue that often arises in group classes. Usually it's a confidence issue. Since copying stems from the belief that one's own ideas aren't as good as those of the other students—or of the movies we watch or the books we read—the worst thing we can do is to make the copied idea off limits. When we do, students dig in their heels and insist they have no ideas at all.

When a group is struggling with too many copied ideas among the group, I often try a silent freewriting game. We might use a general idea, perhaps one I suggest, and students each have five minutes to write a beginning based on the idea. Then, when we share—and each story is unique—students start to discover that ideas can head in many directions. Next, we might turn our attention to the actual idea that has been copied in our class and figure out what direction each of the writers wants to go to make sure they've each found their own territory.

With copied ideas from books or movies, the Act It Out game might be used to explore what might happen if the character in question were in a new setting or facing a new problem. You might try a couple what-ifs and rewind each scene a few times in order to create a collection of possibilities. After stretching the idea in a variety of directions, writers can usually see more possibility and create more original material.

Questions as a Teaching Tool

As in side-coaching, modeling employs many questions. Teaching with questions is an art, and requires a few considerations.

First, we need to be sure we're not asking a question that fishes for a specific answer. Questions are meant to invite. They should invite learners to wonder. We should honestly be wondering when we ask. For instance, "Did anyone notice something new about their characters in the game we just played?" Their answers might lead you to ask, "So, what do we think makes a character seem like a real person?" It's not that we ourselves have no ideas on the topic, but we wonder what this particular class thinks, too. When we list their thoughts on the board, we're likely to be just as surprised as anyone else in class by the thought-provoking way someone expresses an idea.

Second, we need to be sure we aren't manipulating with our questions. Sometimes we might be given a surface-level answer. It's tempting to say, "So are you saying that…" and add our more in-depth answer. But we know the student isn't saying whatever words we just put in his or her mouth. A more constructive way to address such a situation might be to say, "Tell me more about that. What do you mean by…"

Or we might open the discussion up to the group: "Yes, characters do seem more real when they have a favorite food. Why do we think that is?"

Or even, "I agree. Knowing a character loves pizza helps me relate to them. My favorite kind of pizza, for instance, is mushroom and olive. I wonder what kind of pizza my character might like. Maybe Canadian bacon and pineapple. Probably, because she likes sweets. In fact, I think her sweet tooth might be important in my story. Maybe she'll want to have her birthday party at the neighborhood candy shop. And maybe she'll sneak chocolates in the middle of the night and get in trouble." Then, I might open the question back up to the class. "Maybe it's not only knowing what a character's favorite food is that makes them feel real, but having the things they like connect in some logical way. What do you all think? Can anyone give me an example using their own character?"

Third, when we use questions, we have to be open to silence. When no one offers an immediate answer, this isn't a bad thing. Most times, it means the class is thinking. If we jump in to rescue them every time there's a pause, they learn they don't need to think for themselves. Why should they do the work if we're just going to hand them a perfectly packaged answer? After a reasonable pause, we can ask something along the lines of "Are we stumped? What are we puzzling over?" We open the doorway for a discussion of what they're thinking about. Or we can suggest a new, related question: "Maybe another question to ask is…"

Choose a picture book and read it front to back. Then, list the topics a writer might explore through reading this book closely. How is characterization shown? Is there wordplay that works well? How about the structure of the book? Settings? Positive and negative turns? Suspense? Active verbs? Sentence structure? Choose one topic on your list and think through how you'd put into words your thoughts about what the writer is doing well. Take your insights with you into your classroom.

To learn from our favorite writers, we must look past their brilliance to what, specifically, they're doing.

REAL-WORLD EXAMPLES

Specifics are powerful. When we model, either with our own writing or with books, we tell the story of how a writer achieved an effect, which can then lead students to discover how to achieve a similar effect, too.

One excellent way to share our role as a fellow learner is to model reading as a writer. By showing young writers how we identify a strength in a writer's work, how we study that strength, and then how we try it out in our own writing, we open up a vast number of learning opportunities. Every author a young writer admires becomes a potential mentor; each library a treasure trove filled with expertise.

While the process is simple, it's not necessarily intuitive. In order to learn from our favorite writers, we have to see past their brilliance to the specifics of what they are doing. It's easy to say we love a book but much more difficult to put into words why we love it. Usually there are several elements we love in a book, large and small. Narrowing our focus is challenging. We must ignore all the "but I also love…" thoughts that pop up the minute we make a choice and look deeply at one part of the writer's craft.

When we model how to read as a writer, it's a good idea to then give the students a chance to try the skill again right away on their own. Once they've applied the practice of choosing one small element on which to focus, they will be able to do it with more ease the next time around.

Modeling as a Teaching Tool

Throughout history, teachers have used real-world stories as a powerful teaching tool. When we model, we use the story of our work, our thinking, our questions, and our ideas as a case study for our students. It's not that our process then becomes an exact how-to that our students use. Rather, by hearing our story, students see how a strategy or process might play out in one specific instance. Then, it's much easier for them to take that idea and apply it to their own work. Emotional connections are made when we share how frustrated we became trying something out. Students realize that they aren't terrible at writing just because the process doesn't always come easily. Were we to tell them this truth, it wouldn't sink nearly as deep. But when they hear the story of frustration or success from our vantage point, and continue to hear our stories over time, they begin creating a larger picture of what being a writer can mean. With a more open mind, they make discoveries of their own. They notice what we tried and then they make connections and ideas pop to mind. Now, they have strategies of their own and stories of their own experiments, challenges, and successes to tell. Modeling works because we are no longer the teacher who may not understand our students' confusion or frustration. We're fellow travelers, learning right along with our students. Since we are further down the path than they are, we are able to look back over our shoulders and shout warnings about bears that may be around corners, and to call out encouragement about how that steep incline is worth climbing because of the vista ahead. As we become mentors, our experiences become trailmarkers for our charges. The added benefit is that our experiences are given new meaning when seen through our mentees' eyes.

It's important to ask questions to help learners reflect.

TRY THIS...

Start a reader's journal. Choose a book you read recently and analyze it with a "reading as a writer" lens. Write some notes on your thoughts and consider sharing your thoughts with your students.

AND THEN...

Reflect on a mentor you have had. What did your mentor do, specifically, that helped you most? Write out at least one moment, using as many details as you can, to recall the gift of that relationship. Consider turning your writing into a thank-you letter to send to your mentor.

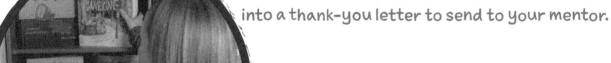

CHAPTER SEVEN

Writerly Chats

———◦———

When we confer, we help writers reflect on their writing and thinking process, rather than just about the story itself. The goal of conferring is to raise a writer's awareness of his or her own writing craft and to empower that writer to choose words, ideas, and strategies with purpose.

→ ONE-MINUTE BRAIN-STRETCH

Imagine you could sit down with one of your favorite authors. Picture where the meeting might take place in your ideal scenario. If you could ask him or her any question about your writing, what might you ask? How do you think the conversation might go from there?

Conferring conversations are short and tightly focused.

PREPARING FOR A CONFERENCE

Conferring is a powerful strategy in which we give each young writer ownership over his or her personal learning journey.

Conferring is a conversation between student and mentor. Sometimes a conference might take place among a group of students, but in most cases conferring happens one-on-one. Ideally, each student will have a chance to confer in nearly every session. For this to be possible, conferring conversations must be kept short and tightly focused. The benefits for the facilitator of keeping conversations short are clear—it's much easier to make one's way around the classroom to speak with all or most students. However, short conferences are also good for our writers. When we have quick conversations, we provide a tidbit or two of instruction and then immediately allow them time to apply the strategy. In this way, students learn to be self-sufficient and continue to own their learning. Ideally, a conferring conversation should last one to three minutes and no more than five.

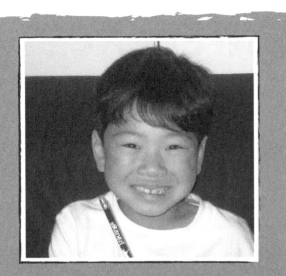

Conferring is more about the writer than it is about the writing itself.

Conferring, Not Editorial Feedback

In conferring conversations, we generally consider a very short portion of a student's writing. These conversations do not require in-depth reading. The purpose of these conversations is not to look at the story as a whole, but rather to identify what a writer is currently doing in his work and to help him focus on a specific skill or strategy. Conferring is more about the writer than it is about the specific writing. The writing is simply the vehicle for the conversation. Conferring makes the discoveries from the games, the focus of the day, and the modeling all practical and applicable to the student's specific learning needs.

When to Confer and When to Wait

Ideally, conferring happens in most Writerly Play sessions. Sometimes students are on a roll, though, and we don't want to interrupt simply to feel as if we're doing our job. Also, we may have students who struggle with their writing and who construct a notebook blockade every time we walk past their desk. These students may not trust us to be part of their writing process yet. In both of these scenarios, it makes sense to skip over a week or two of conferring. For a strong writer, the break provides the opportunity to decide when and why to have a conference. This writer can then come to the conferences with his or her own objective and be squarely in the driver's seat of the learning process. For a reluctant writer, the respite allows trust to build. As facilitators, we're not forcing our way into their fortress. In both cases, I share my objective for the conference clearly: "I want to hear how things are going for you and help you continue to develop your writing skills." Then, I put the power in their court. "I need to have a conference with you this week or next to check in. I'll let you decide whether you'd like it to be today or next week. If you decide you'd like to meet today, just wave me over."

Give Fair Warning

In order to prepare your students for successful conferring conversations, you'll want to give them an overall picture of the interaction ahead of time. Because we're shifting the teacher-student relationship to mentor-mentee, we need to clarify the differences in our relationship, particularly with regard to conferring. We aren't circulating to point out grammar, spelling, or vocabulary problems. Our objective is to help students continue to develop their skills. Some classroom teachers I recently worked with cleverly chose to use different hats while working with their students. One hat signaled that they were in conferring mode. They wore another while sitting at a group table and working with students on mechanics, in order to make a clear, physical distinction about the two roles. This way, they could overtly teach grammar and spelling without concern that this editorial work would muddy their conferring role, in which they talked

with students about strategies, technique, and the big picture.

One way to help demystify conferring is to model a typical writerly conversation. Start with the standard "How's it going?" and help the writer through the process of sharing what's going on. A powerful way to model what makes conferring conversations work is to show what happens when a writer shrugs in response to the question. "How's it going?" (Shrug.) Then, you can turn to the class. "So, I want to help this writer. What do you think she needs?" (No one knows.) So, I continue, "Let's imagine she said, 'I just got started with my scene. I don't think I have any questions yet.' Then, I might say, 'Great! Today we talked about a lot of ways to show details about our characters in the first scene. I'm going to circulate the room and come back later. Maybe we can talk about how you're doing with character details, or maybe you'll have a different question you want to discuss. I'll be back.'"

After this sample dialogue, I might ask the group, "What kinds of questions might a writer bring up in a conferring conversation that would help her?"

They might suggest questions such as, "I'm trying to make this forest seem creepy. Is it working?" or, "I'm not sure what would happen next. I'm kind of lost," or, "I had all these ideas for the scene but now that I'm writing it down, they're all going by kind of fast."

Once students hear their peers sharing ideas for questions, they realize having a question doesn't mean they've made a mistake. In fact, as you explore questions, your students should start to see how coming up with questions and addressing them with their mentor may help improve their stories or their overall writing skills. The first skill we're building—and it's often helpful to share with the students that this skill, too, can be developed—is coming up with thinking and discussion points about our writing in the first place. An observation is just as helpful as a question. For instance, when I ask, "How's it going?" and a student answers, "I just noticed that when I start lines of dialogue mid-sentence, the story speeds up," I want to cheer. What a fantastic opening for a constructive conversation!

→ **TRY THIS!**

Grab a colleague, or if no one else is around, use an imagined colleague. Play out a few possible conferring scenarios. How might the conversation go if the student is feeling silly? Defensive? Talkative? Inspired? Together, brainstorm creative ways to tackle the challenges that may arise.

Ask yourself: What's the next step to help this student grow?

A CONFERRING CONVERSATION

Conferring conversations follow a predictable pattern on which the mentor and mentee can rely.

Using a predictable pattern helps keep conferring conversations short, and allows the student to have equal partnership in the discussion. When they know what to expect, writers can direct the conversation toward what's most on their minds.

Initiating the Conversation

As you circulate, begin your conferring conversations by pulling up next to a writer and asking them some version of "How's it going?" Since you've already modeled this question, writers won't be surprised or put off by the question. In fact, they should have some idea of what to say next. On the first day of conferring, this moment can be handled with humor, too. If a student shrugs or doesn't know what to say, you might provide an idea for what they might say rather than shrugging. Then, rewind your conversation to the beginning and try again. We're working

A TYPICAL CONFERENCE

1. "How's it Going?"

2. Identify a Topic

3. Narrow the Focus

4. Determine a Strategy

5. Name the Strategy

6. Follow Up

on helping students realize they need to have an answer to this question. Their growth as a writer depends on thinking about what they are doing in a bigger-picture way. It's not enough to write this one piece. One must also think about the process of writing, about what they're learning from this project that might be transferable to other projects.

Identify a Topic

Depending on a student's answer to "How's it going?" you have at least three options for your conferring topic.

1. You might address the question, which of course is the best option if the question is meaty enough to launch a conversation.

2. You might read a few sentences of their work and point out something you immediately notice, such as, "I see you're experimenting with dialogue. I like how this makes your

characters start to sound like real people. Can we read this part out loud back and forth?"

3. If you don't see anything immediate as you read a student's work, you can always address the skill of the day. Be careful not to put the writer on the spot. Sometimes students don't immediately apply what was discussed in class that day, particularly if the skill addressed doesn't relate to the given scene. If at all possible, lead with what you see a writer *is* doing, not with pointing out what he or she is not doing. One workaround might be, "So, how far are you through this scene?" Once he answers, you could continue. "Okay, so when you start the new scene, that might be a place to use some of the setting details we explored in our games today. Maybe I'll give you a few minutes to finish this scene and come back when you've had a chance to start the new scene."

When identifying a topic, the question is: What's the next step to help this student grow? We

want to choose a topic that will provide them with a successful experience.

Narrow the Focus

If the topic is as wide as say, dialogue, the way to assure the student of success is to narrow the focus further. That way, instead of asking herself, "Did I succeed with my dialogue?" which would be an impossible question for any writer to answer, she might ask, "Did I succeed in giving each character a way of speaking and stick to it?" The goal is to leave the writer with one practical strategy to try out when you leave.

If, as in the above example, you read the dialogue back and forth, focusing in on a topic might sound like, "I like how your characters are listening to one another and answering each other's questions. Since they're brother and sister, one way to make the characters sound even more realistic might be to have them interrupt each other every once in a while. What do you think?"

If the writer agrees, then the focus might be how to use interruption to make dialogue feel more realistic. If he doesn't agree, ask what else a brother and sister might do when they speak with each other. In the end, you might choose to focus on the strategy of choosing a word or phrase that is unique to one of the characters and using that strategy a few times throughout the scene, or the strategy of adding specific action tags to the dialogue.

The strategy itself isn't as important as the fact that the writer is exerting control over his or her writing. When we become aware that our choices cause particular effects in our writing, we consider all our choices more carefully. As this control grows, we are repositioned with regard to our writing. Our words and ideas no longer appear to us out of the blue as the only option. Instead, what we do with each idea, each sentence, each

character, is all up to us.

Determine a Strategy

Strategies are most helpful when they make the issue in question visible. Most of what we do when we write is subconscious and invisible. We don't know where our ideas come from. We have no idea why we think of pumpkins and tractors on rainy days when we think of a farm, or why our character says, "Bet the sun's coming out any minute," rather than "When will this rain stop?" Eventually any skill we focus on will become subconscious again, but in order to achieve mastery over a particular element of our writing, we need to be able to see it clearly. I still remember learning in second grade that a story could start with dialogue. I felt like a masterful writer because I had conscious control over this one part of my writing. I could start my stories in an interesting way. Probably nothing else about the stories was masterful, but I felt successful. I was making a specific choice in order to achieve a particular effect. I was doing what authors do.

Sometimes it is most efficient to propose a strategy for a student. Many times the strategy can be supported by one of the worksheets or by a pencil and paper activity. Ultimately, we're moving students toward being ready to collaborate with us to invent a custom strategy. To provide steppingstones toward this ability, we might share a way we have addressed this particular issue and then ask the student to think about a strategy of his own. Often, the student will adapt the presented strategy, adding his own flair.

When you're showing a student how to apply a strategy, use words from what he or she has written, pointing out what the student has already done well. Remember, there is a difference between helping students stand on the shoulders of what they have already done in order to build their skills, and pointing out their flaws. Similar conversations, different outcomes.

Name the Strategy

Before leaving the conferring conversation, it's ideal to name the strategy, particularly if you've invented or adapted one together. Naming the strategy makes it feel like something tangible, and sometimes even feels as though you've invented a tiny game. I like to have a log of these strategies, so I keep a binder with one conferring sheet per writer with my Writerly Play teaching materials. Basically, these conferring sheets are blank tables with three columns. I record the date of each conference, the strategy we named, and any additional notes. By tracking our conversations, I can refer to them from week to week and keep track of which writers I may not have chatted with recently.

If the strategy is more standard or worksheet based, I might write it down after leaving the writer's desk. However, keep in mind: the more you involve writers in the recording process, the more control they feel over their own learning.

Follow Up

After the conference, if you think it will be encouraging, circle back to note where students have applied their strategies. In some cases, explaining the strategy or discoveries with the larger group during sharing time will help the class learn and allow the writer to be the group's expert on the topic. When you return for a future conference, refer back to what you did together, where you see it showing up in the student's work currently, and then move on to a new topic.

TRY THIS...

Find a piece of your own (adult) writing you haven't looked at for a while. Read it over objectively, and then script a conferring conversation for yourself. Play both the mentor and the mentee. "How's it going?" "Well, I'm working on..." and so on. You might be surprised with what you discover.

AND THEN...

Think of a time when someone's feedback on your writing made you feel empowered. List the elements of that conversation. Then, think of a time when feedback stopped you in your tracks. Record the elements of that feedback as well. Compare lists. What do you notice?

Taming *the* Storm

---◇---

Set up your class well, and every session to follow will benefit.

Classroom management is a dance between preparation and

adjustment, based on the needs of the day. Just as in all aspects

of a Writerly Play workshop, students should take ownership for

their class running smoothly. Cast the vision for how a smooth

session looks and empower students to help make it happen.

Think back to the last event at which you felt truly comfortable. What did you encounter as you entered the space? What did it sound like? Look like? What elements of the experience caused you to feel welcome? How might you create a similar space in your Writerly Play workshop, particularly on a first day?

Make the room comfortable, colorful, and welcoming.

A WELL-STRUCTURED WORKSHOP

Classroom management begins before the first student walks in the door on the first day of class.

Consider yourself the host of this party, and your students the guests. Before they arrive, do a strategic sweep of the classroom, moving anything that might be distracting or in the way. Set out pencils, workbooks, and other materials in an inviting manner. To the extent the space allows, make the room comfortable, colorful, and welcoming.

When students arrive, greet them at the door, make them a name tag so everyone can learn one another's name, and show them where to leave their belongings. Then, give them somewhere to go and something to do while the others arrive and settle in.

When you are ready to start, use the opening ritual to set the tone. Then cast your vision for the workshop by sharing what's at the heart of this particular curriculum. Invite your students to dream about what kind of story, poem, or piece of writing they may create. Explain what a basic class will look like, provide the framework with your general expectations, and then play a game to get to know one another.

Now, your students feel at home and they're ready to play.

The Safety of Structure

Boundaries in our classrooms are just as important as rules in the games. Creativity flourishes in a safe space. I read recently about a playground near a busy street. For a long time, the children played in a small ring around the building, using only a quarter of the grassy area. Then a fence was installed, ringing the property, defining the line between traffic and playing area. Just like that, the kids spread out, enjoying the freedom to run and explore. Boundaries gave the children more space, not less.

We do our students a disservice when we avoid setting up or enforcing classroom guidelines. Yes, we have the role of mentor, but in a group setting that role includes being the authority figure. By no means must we nor should we be authoritarian, but we do need to hold our students accountable to the guidelines we've set.

The best way to set up class guidelines is for the group to agree on them on the first day. Since many Writerly Play classes are tight on time, the alternative is to use the basic rules with which most students are familiar. These are: Respect yourself, others, and the classroom space. When

you set workshop expectations on the first day, mention these or the guidelines of your choice. By stating your standards up front, you give your class a framework within which to play. If, later, you need to discuss behavior with a student, your expectations won't come out of left field.

Theatre games require additional boundaries, since students may not be familiar with how best to play. Before you launch into any theatre game, it's important to establish any guidelines for the game in a clear, concise way. For most movement games, this means defining the basic boundaries of the playing space, reminding players that they should avoid touching other players or items in the space, and clarifying whether this is a speaking or silent game.

Make Structure a Game

One of the beauties of the Writerly Play approach is that the students are on their toes and ready to play. Classroom management can be rolled into the game. When we use a countdown to transition from desks to the carpet area, the focus is on making it to the circle on time rather than on following rules. We might use freeze or Slo-Mo or Full-Body Whisper at any time to bring bodies and voices back under reasonable control.

For a class with a particular management challenge—maybe the students are overly talkative or physical—create a game together to manage the situation. Maybe you have a special kind of freeze with a code word—say, pickle—that requires everyone to stand up, jump up and down three times, and then make a silly pose. You won't have to say, "Stop touching one another, sit down, be careful, stop running, no wrestling…" ad infinitum. Instead, you'll say "pickle" and rather than having frustrated, annoyed students, you'll have a class of laughing, engaged ones.

Anticipation

A large part of keeping your class on track is anticipating what might go wrong and front-loading a few strategic guidelines before starting an activity. If there's a stack of toys on a shelf because this room doubles as a preschool classroom, point them out and state your expectations before kids start grabbing them. If you're a classroom teacher leading Writerly Play in your usual classroom, think through any areas you may want to close prior to play, such as the book corner or other centers.

If you have two students who notoriously can't stand close without dive-tackling each other, state clearly that you expect them to place themselves at a distance from each other even as they move around the room.

Be aware that when kids are sitting in a circle or at their desks, you have more control and more of their attention than you'll have when they stand up and start moving. Give important guidelines and set boundaries *before* your students move.

Similarly, when students each stand on an X, you have more control than when they stand wherever they choose. If your class has difficulty with movement games, an easy workaround is to use masking tape X's or carpet squares. Start with simple poses and controlled movement within a defined space. Next, loosen the boundaries by allowing movement from one spot to another. Then, when players are able to control their bodies within this framework, experiment with longer periods of movement before asking players to find their way back to their spots. Each return to the safety of the designated spot allows players to take a breath and reset their energy. The renewed focus also allows facilitators to give instructions that they're sure will be heard.

Clarity and Consistency

While our goal in the games is sometimes to keep students off balance and guessing, our goal with classroom management is the opposite. Students

Give important guidelines and set boundaries before your students move around the room.

should clearly understand our expectations. If one day we allow wrestling and another day we do not, we lose our credibility. If we tell a student that if they throw another pencil they will need to sit out, and then we don't follow through, we lessen the power of any other statement we might make. When we don't keep our word, students learn that our boundaries might be firm or they might not. This lack of clarity undermines our effectiveness.

Consistency is difficult when it comes to power struggles, and particularly so in teaching situations outside the normal boundaries of the school day. If we're teaching after school, for instance, we need to be doubly careful about setting ultimatums. When an ultimatum is broken, and we need to enforce the rule, but we don't have a principal's office to which to send students, it can feel as though our hands are tied. For instance, we warn a student that if they knock into their friend again, they will need to sit out of the game. Then, they knock into their friend again. We direct the student to sit out and they refuse.

Now what? If we'e going to remain consistent, our only real option is to stop the game, redirect all the players into chairs for their safety, and let the student who has refused to follow the rules know that we will speak with their parent about the behavior after class. Now, we've moved into consequences that might ultimately lead to the student being removed from class.

Say we're reasonably sure a student will not be able to keep from knocking into her friend. Say we've also seen a stubborn streak in her. What if, instead of setting up the ultimatum at all, we morph the game into a shape in which it will be nearly impossible for anyone to knock into anyone? For instance, instead of moving around the room, we set down masking tape X's and do the game in a more controlled way. While this creates a limitation for the full class, rather than just the one student, it also bypasses a power struggle. After the game we can discuss how the class can work toward earning full movement around the classroom. Then students can set their own goals, which will be much more powerful than another nag on our part about not knocking into our friends.

The other way to avoid ultimatums is to present the player with an either/or option. You've avoided the initial power struggle by giving them the choice, but there is always the danger that they'll refuse either option. For students with whom we've established rapport, though, an either/or option generally works well.

Ideally, we should avoid ultimatums as much as we can, particularly if we're not sure yet if the students respect us enough to take them to heart. If you are teaching an extracurricular Writerly Play workshop, you don't have as much time as a classroom teacher to develop that kind of respect. If this situation is your reality, it is even more important to rely on the games—and the joyful structure they can bring—as your primary tool for classroom management.

For classroom teachers who employ Writerly Play in their rooms, transitions are particularly important. The opening ritual is essential to create a clear transition into the rules of our Writerly

Play work, which are likely different than the guidelines of the regular school day. At the end of the lesson, during sharing, a classroom teacher might want to close the workshop with a simple structured activity to help students transition back to their normal classroom routine.

No matter what time of day or format in which you teach your Writerly Play workshop, the best-case scenario is to avoid standoffs with students wherever possible. Ideally, keep the class moving in such a lively way that writers can't help but stay engaged.

→ TRY THIS!

Play with the idea of hosting a mischievous character from literature in your classroom. What might Ramona do in your classroom? Or Gilly Hopkins? Or Huck Finn? What sort of structure might you set up in anticipation of the kinds of trouble that might be coming your way?

Grab a deck of index cards. One on side of each card, write a classroom management scenario that might come up in a Writerly Play workshop. List situations, one per card, for two minutes. Then, set the timer for three minutes and write possible strategies for fixing the challenges on the flip side of each card.

Young writers need to know we'll keep them safe—socially, physically, and creatively.

ᴬ STRATEGY TOOLKIT

There are a variety of tried-and-true strategies that help classrooms run smoothly. Here are a few to consider adding to your Writerly Play toolkit.

Ultimately, we want our students to be so engaged with the games and the writing that behavior is something they manage themselves. However, while it may feel intuitive to come to class with a "we're all on the same team" attitude, that approach can sometimes backfire. Young writers need to know the limitations and that we'll keep them safe—socially, physically, and creatively. Often, much of the groundwork for this understanding has already been laid by excellent educators before us. When our writers hear us using words and methods they've heard from other trusted teachers, they relax, realizing that we speak the language of teachers, too. Once we've established our leadership in the classroom, we can also move toward establishing our mentorship dynamic as another layer in our relationship with the writers.

Here's how I think about this dynamic. For group facilitation, I'm a teacher. In every individual

One of the simplest ways to make work into a game is to set a time limit.

interaction, I'm a mentor. When I need my teacher self to protect the space and advocate for the students, I often employ one or more of the following strategies.

Transition Warnings

One of the simplest ways to make work into a game is to set a time limit. Writing a paragraph on cows might be a chore, but writing a paragraph on cows before the timer dings is a game. Now the question is not "What should I write?" but rather "Will I get my writing done on time?" If we add another challenge—say, that no word in our paragraph can be more than five letters long—we raise the game's stakes higher still.

In the midst of a creative process, transitions are often an emotional hot spot. One gets on a roll and then the facilitator asks the group to stop. Maybe this writer looks around and realizes that everyone else has filled out the entire worksheet or completed a full page of writing, but she hasn't. She feels behind and as though she has failed. The challenge for a facilitator is keeping the pace of class lively without causing this kind of frustration. Nothing drains the energy out of a room more than a number of writers being done and then waiting around with nothing to do other than distracting the others.

Anticipate these challenges by setting a time limit that will push writers to make quicker decisions than they might normally, but that will also give them enough time to think. Then, when you are about a minute out from the limit, warn the class that time is running short. If many writers seem to need more time, offer an extra minute or two. If many writers seem close to finishing, remind the group that they don't need to be finished with their worksheet or the page of writing. They can always come back to it later. When there are only twenty or thirty seconds left, ask the students to finish their thoughts and then put their pencils down. These warnings allow the writers to renegotiate their personal expectations along the way instead of facing their frustration all at once when the time is up.

The same goes for other transitions. Warnings always help, whether they are for the final moments of a game, the final moments of a sharing time, or the end of a break. When we give our students advance notice, we give them the power to make decisions with the time they have, rather than making them feel as though what happens in the workshop is completely out of their control.

Dealing with Frustration

We all have days when our emotions are closer to the surface than others. Students have a knack

for sniffing out these days and setting upon us like packs of monkeys, pushing all our buttons. When frustration strikes, it's important to be honest with ourselves. Maybe the plan for the day includes a number of challenging games. We start in, but within minutes have a pounding headache. Part of classroom management is knowing when not to set up battles in the first place. Maybe today is a day to sit back down in a circle, to give a quick mini-lesson on the topic of the day, practice it by telling a story sentence by sentence, and then send the students off to write. For those students who might resist writing, maybe we bring out colored pencils and plot planning sheets and ask them to draw out their story plan instead.

The questions to ask ourselves on such a day as this are:

1. What objective(s) must I meet today?
2. What can I let go today?
3. What is the path of least resistance toward reaching my objective(s)?

Often our workshops are shorter than we like. We put pressure on ourselves to use every bit of our time perfectly. It's difficult to remember to give ourselves grace. Set yourself and your students up for success by being kind, practical, and realistic with yourself.

Class Meetings

When disruptive behavior isn't isolated to one or two students, it's important to give the full class a role in solving the problem. Where you may have started class with just the simple expectations, now more clarification is needed. The group needs a class meeting. What's fantastic about class meetings is that the group can brainstorm the ideal classroom together and then come up with a plan for how to create that environment. Everyone is empowered to help, and no one is called out or individually blamed for the problem. Unlike a who's-at-fault conversation, the results are proactive and much more efficient.

Also, keep in mind that students are highly sensitive to fairness. Often it is not the loudest student who initiated the problem; they're just the one we noticed. Whenever we take the side of one and ignore what the other has done, we lose credibility and trust. Class meetings make establishing firmer guidelines going forward less personal. When students aren't defensive, they're much more likely to jump on board with the new boundaries.

On this note, too, be very careful about calling someone out. Turn group discussions away from the specific "John needs to stop..." to the more general "We all need to keep our hands in our own space." Never call out a student in front of other kids in a way that humiliates or shames him. The natural "What were you thinking?" reaction only breeds resentment and dissolves trust. Whether it is in the group meeting or an individual conversation, make sure to avoid focusing on one student when others are watching. Pull a student aside when a one-on-one discussion is required.

School Language

Many schools use the metaphor of filling buckets to address respect. Are we filling a friend's bucket or dumping their bucket out? For those facilitators who aren't classroom teachers, but who are visitors on school campuses, learning a few of these overall school management catch phrases can make discussing expectations much more simple.

Also, most schools employ a standard conversation for one-on-one conflict resolution. The most typical is the *I feel* conversation. Rather than engaging in a he-did, she-did kind of conversation, teachers facilitate a conversation along the lines of:

When you (specific disruptive behavior, no emotional interpretations), **I feel** (emotion) **because** (reason), **so what I would like is** (the change desired).

Often both students need to use this format, because both are frustrated and feel unheard. Keep in mind that forced apologies or promises at this moment are often empty. Instead, a more honest question might be, "Jack, what can you agree to?" and then, "Lisa, what can you agree to?" and then, "Do we both feel satisfied with this agreement?" If the answer is no, keep at it or agree to take some time to cool off and think, and then discuss it again before the end of the class. Make sure not to leave an argument unresolved when students leave for the day. If nothing else, leave with an agreement for how to address the situation when they come back for the next session.

→ THREE-MINUTE BRAIN-STRETCH

Fold a paper in half lengthwise. Set a timer for 90 seconds. On one side of the page, list out-of-this-world rewards that you'd love to give your class. A hot-air balloon ride across the country, the ability to make three wishes as a class (and what do you think they'd wish?) or maybe granting the power of flight for an hour. What kind of reward would feel magical to give? Then, when the time's up, turn the paper over. For the next 90 seconds list some rewards that you could actually give to your students. How did listing impossible rewards first affect the quality of this new list? For me, the wild brainstorm sometimes rattles new possibilities loose.

Providing a reward puts focus on positive behavior instead of highlighting the negative.

REWARDS AND CONSEQUENCES

Sometimes, the behavior of a class or student can't be redirected. Then, we have to use rewards and or consequences in order to establish the safe, creative environment that writers need.

Ideally, students are motivated to participate in class and to write because they are excited about the stories or ideas they are communicating on the page. In some cases, due to various factors, our young writers need more motivation.

Individual/Class Rewards

When I'm writing a particularly challenging piece or pushing toward a large deadline, I find that sometimes an external reward mid-process is helpful. The reward of the completed book might be too far off to motivate me day in and day out. Maybe I reward myself for a hard day's work with a window-shopping trip in one of my favorite neighborhoods or a walk on a beautiful trail. Maybe I give myself permission to pick up that new novel I've been wanting to read after I write a certain number of words. Nearly every day, I reward myself for writing by adding a check mark to an app that records my progress. I see the days pile up with win after win. Keeping my commitment to myself makes me feel proud. Each day, I build a longer streak I don't want to break.

We can replicate this experience for our students, either as individuals or as a full class. We can use a jar of jelly beans—if we fill the jar, we earn a group reward such as fun pencils for everyone or a special snack. We can reward individual writers with stickers on days when they do great work, or give the class an extra game at the end of a session if they focus particularly well.

For groups who need extra help with focus and self-control, providing a reward allows the facilitator to publicly appreciate the positive behavior rather than always pointing out the negative. The benefits of this approach are obvious, but note also that when we give attention to something, positive or negative, it multiplies. If we use a positive reward rather than punishment as our

primary behavior management tool, our classroom environment will be much more enjoyable for all.

Audience Chair

One of the most effective consequences in a theatre game is the audience chair. The games are so fun that no one wants to sit out for long. Ideally, the audience chair can be set up as a place when no one is technically in trouble. Players might sit out a round after they lose a challenge in a game. If the game is stimulating enough, it will offer the opportunity for all to win some and lose some. This way, you can cycle through the game, giving all players opportunities to win and to lose. Thus, the audience chair loses its power of humiliation. It's just a place to sit out a round until it's time to get back into the game. Once you've established the audience chair, you can also use it when someone needs to sit out a round for another reason, such as to regain control of their body or voice. Now, the player doesn't have to fight through shame to get to the point where he can adjust his behavior and rejoin the game.

The best way to send someone to the audience chair is with a quick tap on the shoulder and an instruction. Move immediately away and on with the game. The less attention on the disruptive player, the better. No need to watch to make sure they go to the chair. They can't get back into the game until they sit out, so it's in their best interest to sit and wrangle themselves back into control. After they have done so, they can be tapped back into the game. Make sure to be consistent about tapping players back in quickly, too, so the chair functions more as a focusing tool rather than a punishment.

Talking with Parents

In many Writerly Play workshops, we won't have the typical school consequences at our disposal—missing recess, the principal's office, and so forth—and so, often our only consequence above and beyond pulling a child out of an activity is to address the problem with parents. Using a parent conversation as a consequence puts the mentor-mentee relationship at risk, and so the conversation must be handled carefully.

First, give the student the chance to avoid such a conversation. Give at least one warning during class that you may need to talk to their parent if the behavior continues. If what happens is on-the-spot unacceptable and must be addressed with a parent regardless, give the student the opportunity to improve his or her behavior in the remainder of the class time. This way, you will also be able to share how the student worked hard to modify behavior after the incident and put a positive spin on the situation.

Second, when you do speak with the parent, include the student in the conversation. Nothing is worse than being talked about behind your back. Explain what happened objectively and what your expectations are for the future. Then, share anything else you noticed in class, particularly any observation of productive behavior. Have an honest conversation with student and parent about whether the student wishes to continue in class. Discuss the options based on what the student says. Ideally, your class has a written behavior policy to which you can refer as part of this discussion. Maybe there are two warnings after which a student is removed from class. Be firm, official, and clear about this policy while also offering the warm hope that next week will be much more fun for all.

Third, follow up with an email to reinforce what you discussed. Seeing the expectations and your encouragement for their child in writing will show parents you're invested in their child's success and will complete the encounter with a positive tone.

TRY THIS...

Brainstorm a positive reward that might work in your next Writerly Play class. Think about whether you'd prefer to offer a group reward or individual ones,. Then consider what creative spin you might put on this challenge and reward to fit the group or the theme of the class.

AND THEN...

Think of a time when a teacher had to correct your behavior. Was it a productive interaction? If it was, write about what worked for you. If not, rewrite the scene, scripting it the way it might have worked better.

GO FORTH AND PLAY!

WHAT'S NEXT?

Maybe you've been teaching and trying out these strategies all along as you've been playing your way through this book. If you haven't, now is the time to dip your toe in the water. Try out just one game, maybe one that feels easy and safe to you. Build your side-coaching skills.

Gather a group of colleagues and host a game night, swapping out as the facilitator so everyone has a chance to lead. Like backflips and the butterfly stroke, at some point with Writerly Play, one must take the leap and see what happens. Treat each game as an experiment. The more playful your approach to facilitation, the more your charges will be able to relax and play along with you.

In the final pages of this book, you'll find detailed descriptions of the games and a list of conferring topics. Also, don't forget about the downloads and resources waiting for you at www.writerlyplay.com.

Remember, Writerly Play is an approach to developing as a writer. Writerly Play makes the writing process visible, concrete, and manageable. We hope that Writerly Play has already helped YOU develop your writing stamina, courage, and skill. As our community has grown, one of the most exciting developments has been how each new Writerly Play-er brings new layers, creativity, and perspective to the work. Now, as you continue on your journey, we look forward to seeing how your experimentation and play will add to the conversation.

Here's to all the possibilities!

Game Index

—————◇—————

Use this collection of games as a starting place. All these games can be reshaped into many forms with many purposes. As you become more adept with using games, you'll find yourself inventing your own, which is all part of the fun.

A COLLECTION OF GAMES

As you've seen, the games are the heart of Writerly Play. Each lesson adapts and applies these games differently, and we're inventing new games all the time. We hope you will, too!

There is nothing magic about these particular games. However, this is a collection of games that work well to help writers analyze the elements of stories, poems, or nonfiction. These games also work well to help writers plan and revise their work. Many other theatre, movement and visualization games can also be adapted or invented for Writerly Play. Approach this collection of games with a spirit of innovation. Adaptation often takes into account the size of the group. One-on-one, the games look different, of course, but they also change in large groups for logistical reasons. Games also change shape and focus according to the age and experience level of the players.

Writerly Play games shouldn't be viewed as a sequence of activities to use once and then move on to the next. Instead, they are more like yoga poses or fitness activities. Once a player understands the basics of a game, he or she can then push further, add nuances, and use the games as tools to explore new stories, ideas, and layers of skill.

There is one consideration to keep in mind when adding new games to this collection. Most theatre games are designed with performance as the end goal. In our case, the direction is flipped on its head. Performance and/or devising a group story is almost never the destination. The ultimate plan is that each writer will create an individual work of art. When doing group work or performance games, work toward exploring the story concepts through the group example, and then encourage students to take the concept and apply it to their own ideas.

Circle Games

There are countless theatre games played in a circle. Here are a few that are fun warm-ups. These games encourage quick response and build energy for a session of games, or help players regroup when they have lost focus. Circle games are an excellent place to practice celebrating mistakes, a concept that carries over into the attitude for writing. When working on the skill of celebrating mistakes, I will often ask the group to strike silly poses and/or say a silly word together each time a mistake is made. This process transforms the moment of the mistake into a funny group experience.

With a little creative thinking, most of these games can be adapted for one-on-one situations, but in those cases, these games look and feel more like quick-thinking games.

1-2-3-4-5

One player stands in the middle of the circle. She calls out a title and points to one player in the circle. That player and the person on his/her right and left must make a specific picture and a specific noise before the person in the middle counts to five. Below are a few titles that can be used.

Angels: The middle player puts her hands together. The players on either side turn their backs toward the center player and strum their harps. Together, they sing, "Ahhh..."

Elvis: The middle player sings into a microphone. The player on the right plays guitar and the player on the left plays piano. Together, they sing, "Well-a, Well-a."

Jell-O: The middle player puts his arms in the air and jiggles. The two outside players make a bowl with their hands. They all make jiggly noises.

Washing Machine: The middle player puts his fists together and swishes back and forth. The players on either side put their arms together and make the outside of the machine. They all make swish noises.

Elephant: The middle player uses her arms to make the nose of the elephant, and the players on either side make the ears. All trumpet like an elephant.

BIPPITY-BOP-BOP-BOP

The players stand in a circle with one player in the middle. The middle player moves to one of

the players on the outside of the circle and says, "Bippity-bop-bop-bop," as fast as she can. The chosen player must say bop before the middle player finishes the phrase. The middle player can be tricky. She can say "bop" to a player on the outside of the circle, or give a false start. Players end up in the middle if they say bop too late, if they say bop before the middle player says bippity, or if they say bop when the middle player says nothing at all. The middle player stays in the middle until someone on the outside makes a mistake.

EIGHT-COUNT SHAKEDOWN

In a circle, ask each writer to raise a foot. As a group, the players shake their feet eight times while counting aloud. Shake the other foot eight times. Then shake one hand eight times, and then the other hand. Repeat the pattern, this time shaking only seven times, and so on, down to one. Increase speed with each round.

NAME TOSS

Using an imaginary ball, the facilitator tosses her name across the circle to another player. For instance, I would say, "Naomi," as I toss with a clear motion, making eye contact with the player to whom I'm tossing. The person who catches my name passes his name to another player. The goal in this game is to build energy and focus. One way to do this is to keep the players on their toes by introducing calls such as "Plane overhead" and "Full-body whisper" with this game. Also, challenge the group to play a "hot-potato" round, in which they push themselves to catch and toss more quickly.

Variation

With groups who already know one another, players might pass words other than their names, such as their favorite animal, color, or nickname.

PASS A SOUND AND MOTION

Pass a large sound and motion to the player on your left. She passes exactly what she saw and heard to the next person, and around goes the sound and motion. Work on building energy. Once the sound and motion return to the facilitator, pass the sound to the person on your left again, who begins a new sound and motion. Play enough rounds so each person can start the action.

PASS THE CLAP

Turn to your neighbor and together clap at the exact same time. Then, the new player passes the clap to his neighbor, and the clap is passed around the circle. Send the clap all the way around the circle to establish a rhythm. Then, mix it up by allowing players to pass the clap on, or send it back the opposite way. To reverse the direction, a player claps once with his or her neighbor to receive the rhythm, and then catches that same neighbor's eye and claps again together to pass it back.

PATTERNS

Give a category, such as types of foods, colors, or types of candy. One player chooses an item in the category and points to another player. That player chooses an item and points to a new player. Repeat the process until each player has been chosen. This is the first pattern. Try going through the pattern again and begin to speed up. Add difficulty by adding another category or two (so that more than one pattern is going at the same time) or by dropping the pointing and only allowing players to use eye contact to pass the pattern. The goal is to concentrate as a group and keep the pattern(s) going.

THANK-YOU POSE

The facilitator walks to the middle of the circle and freezes in a pose. A second player must join the facilitator, freezing in a complementary pose. The facilitator says, "Thank you," and returns to the outer ring. The second player remains frozen in the center of the circle. Now, a third player enter the circle to pose with the second player. The second player says, "Thank you," and returns to the outer ring. The game continues in this pattern.

YES

One player points across the circle at another player. This gesture is a silent request for that player's spot. The player who is pointed to says, "Yes!" She must then point to someone else and get a spot for herself before the original player reaches her spot. Remind the players to say yes with enthusiasm or at least motivation. The goal in this game is to get this movement going as fast as possible.

Variations

Use this game to review names. Instead of pointing and waiting for a yes, the first player should call out another player's name. Then, the first player heads to the named person's place. The displaced player must call another name before she can leave her spot. Or for even more challenge, use main-character names.

ZIP-ZAP-ZOP

One player points across the circle and passes "zip." The receiver passes "zap" and the next receiver passes "zop." This pattern is repeated until someone makes a mistake. The objective is to speed up the reactions until the game is moving quickly and building group energy.

ZOOM-MOOZ

Begin the game by turning to your neighbor and passing the word "zoom!" The word zoom then passes from player to player clockwise. After zoom has passed all the way around the circle clockwise, try the other direction, as "mooz.". Pass "mooz" counterclockwise from player to player. Next, mix things up. Players can pass "zoom" clockwise, or switch the direction of play and pass "mooz" counterclockwise. Overall, players are trying not to become confused and pass a word in the wrong direction. Build toward quick play to make the game fun. When players make a mistake, pull them out of the game for the round and eliminate down to two players. Nearly all groups will want to play again!

CIRCLE GAME MIX-UP

Play this game after the students know a number of circle games such as Zip-Zap-Zop, Yes, Zoom-Mooz, and Bippity Bop-Bop-Bop. Then, mix all the circle games together for one wild game. Call new games every one or two minutes, keeping the players off balance. Work toward quick, smooth transitions. Eventually, challenge the players to switch on their own. When one player has the game's focus—for instance, he is the player in the middle—he switches the game, and the group changes with him. The goal of the game is to transition seamlessly as a group without losing focus.

Movement Games

These games can help explore setting, character, emotion, description, and active verbs among other things. They are structures that help students explore physically while listening and responding to side-coaching.

In nearly every movement game, you'll want to begin by asking the players to walk in a variety of playful ways. Start with basic movement and build toward imaginative movement in order to build a safe risk-taking environment. Here's a list of movements to get you started:

Move:
- In zig zag lines
- In curving lines
- In polka dots

- As if your body is a giant rubber band
- As if there is suddenly too much gravity
- As if there is too little gravity and you can barely keep your feet on the ground
- As if you're barefoot on hot sand
- As if you're balancing on a beam
- As if you're wearing tennis shoes on an ice-rink
- As if you're knee-deep in jelly beans
- As if you're wading in a swamp
- As if you're tiptoeing through a magical forest
- As if you're trying not to show it, but you think someone is following you

Movement games can be played in one-on-one settings, depending on the space of the session and the personality of the writer. I find that when I ask my mentees to move around the room, they're most comfortable if I move, too. This means I must split my attention between facilitating and moving. Note that when I do this, my movement isn't usually more than skin-deep. I can't think about my story and characters while also facilitating the game. In these cases, my movement is meant to create more privacy for my student.

BUILD A SETTING

First, ask the players to move around the room using creative types of movement to transition into a playful state. Once the players have become involved in the game, they should each choose a setting. Often it is helpful to picture a doorway through which they will walk. When they enter, they should describe (out loud) all the items in the environment—all sides—the ceiling, floor, and four walls, and any other items. Coach the players to use their hands to shape whatever they are describing in space, creating it with words and with their hands. They should stick with one detail and describe it as fully as possible before moving on to the next.

Some common uses for this game in Writerly Play:

Characterization: Explore a space that is important to the character to learn more about the character's personality, tastes, interests, and dislikes.

Setting Exploration: Players choose a setting from their story about which they need to learn more.

CHARACTER LAYER

Begin by asking the players to move around the space. Call "freeze." Do this a few times quickly and use creative types of movement to transition into a playful state. Once the players have become involved in the game, begin to add the character layer by layer. Use prompts to help the writers build their characters from shoes to legs to torso to hands to posture to face. Once they are in character, use the opportunity for players to act as the character in a setting. Use settings from the story, familiar settings, unfamiliar settings, comfortable settings, uncomfortable settings, a space where the character practices a specific skill, a space where the character relaxes, and so on.

FREEZE TAG/SCENE TAG

This game moves players around the space quickly, but in a controlled way. It chases after the group. At the moment a tag is made, the entire group must freeze. Then when the new *It* begins to run, the rest of the group can move again as well. Players are called out if they don't play the game. If, for instance, they don't run away, or don't freeze, or don't try to tag, they are out. Players should be out for only one round of tag and then be sent back into the game. Once the group is successful at freezing the moment each tag is made, incorporate one of the elements below that takes the game to the next level.

Some common uses for this game in Writerly Play:

Wordplay: When the tag is made, It calls out an adjective and the player who was tagged must spontaneously add a noun.

Character Exploration: When It makes the tag, he (or the facilitator) calls out a question to which the person tagged must quickly respond. For example, what color would your character paint his room?

Exploring and Understanding Dialogue: When It makes the tag, the facilitator calls out a scenario and the two players play out a scene first in action, then adding dialogue.

WALK AS IF

Begin by asking the players to move around the room the way they normally walk. Call "freeze." Do this a few times quickly to catch the players off guard. Challenge players to fill any empty spaces with their bodies. You might say, "Don't let any part of our playing space become lonely." Once the players have become involved in the game, move into side-coaching that explores the topic of the session.

Some common uses for this game in Writerly Play:

Laban Movement: Explore Laban's movement words: Float, Punch, Glide, Slash, Dab, Wring, Flick, and Press, and then use one of those movements as the basis for creating a character.

Sensory Exploration: Ask questions to help the players explore sensory description in a setting. Either explore one setting together, such as a forest, or have each player choose his or her own setting and ask bigger-picture questions that would apply in various situations. I generally ask players to choose one outdoor space and then an indoor one so that the prompts can have a little more focus and still apply across the group.

Idea Generation: One way to use Walk as If for idea generation is to ask writers to walk as if they feel a specific way, such as lonely. Then encourage the players to remember a time they felt this way. Ideas can also be generated by asking the players to walk as if they are in a particular setting—for instance, on the moon—and then asking them to think of what might happen next. What would they see, smell, and so on?

Quick-Thinking Games

Like circle games, quick-thinking games unlock creativity and build spontaneity. These skills help writers enter an environment of play, opening access to ideas and inspiration. Quick decision-making is important for writers in many ways. Quick decision-makers can easily move past blocks, take risks, dive in, and "just try" things.

Quick-Thinking games are easily adapted to one-on-one situations. Keep in mind that when movement is involved in a game, the brain functions differently and tends to respond more spontaneously. For this reason, it is sometimes a good idea to add an element of movement to these games, even when they are played in small settings.

CHOCOLATE RIVER

Give each player a piece of newspaper—this is their marshmallow. The facilitator plays the "marshmallow monster," who is absolutely starving for marshmallows. The players must cross the room from one corner to the opposite one, only stepping on newspapers. The marshmallow monster can steal newspapers if they rip, or if anyone sets their paper down on the floor without putting a hand or foot on it. The players' job is to get all the class members across the room without anyone being left behind or falling in the river. If they step in the river, they turn into marshmallow monsters.

Make this game harder by allowing only one player to talk, and taking away papers if others speak, or by giving one paper per two people. If players get stuck, offer them the option of giving up a right, such as the right to speak or the right to use one of their feet—they must hop on one foot the rest of the way—in exchange for a new marshmallow. Use this game to explore the concept of raising the stakes, and to build class unity.

CHOICES

Gather the group in a clump in the center of the room. The facilitator calls out two options, pointing to one side of the room for one and the other side of the room for the second. Players must move to the side they choose. This game works better when players don't explain each choice out loud. I find it's a good idea to give the players a few chances during the game to share the reasons for their choices.

NOTE: This game is much more playful when speed is a factor. Even adding a quick countdown (5-4-3-2-1...) can add to the fun of the game.

Some common uses for this game in Writerly Play:
Characterization: Players make the choices their characters would.

Idea Generation: Players make choices based on their own preferences and explore story ideas based on their ideas, opinions, experiences, and so on.

DID YOU HEAR?

Ask the group to split in half and stand in two single-file lines facing a large space in the middle of the room. The first player in each line runs to the center, and one says (in character), "Did you hear…" and adds some piece of gossip, and the other responds with, "I know…" and adds some detail to what the other player said. After they are done, they run to the end of their lines. After the entire line of players has had a turn, switch the lines so the other side says, "Did you hear…" and the other side says, "I know…"

To provide some structure for this game, try choosing a topic around which to gossip, such as a familiar fairy tale or a random topic such as cheese. Keep in mind that whatever is said doesn't have to be true—just something on which the other player can build. The larger than life the gossip, the better.

DOUBLE BUBBLE

This no-talking game is good for working on body control, concentration, and cooperation. Pair the students in partners. They must choose (without speaking) a way of moving together, such as hopping on one foot, skipping, clapping hands, and so on. Then, while teams are moving around performing their actions, the facilitator calls "double bubble." Each pair must join with another pair and silently decide how they will all move. This pattern continues with groups getting progressively larger until the group is finally in one large circle. Can they all move together in the same way? Call freeze to end the game.

Variations

For a beginning group, instead of making larger and larger bubbles each time you call double bubble, try asking the players to simply switch partners on each double bubble. For an advanced group, call "bubble up" when you want students to switch partners and "double bubble" when you want groups to combine with other groups. Keep them on their toes by mixing up the calls.

I HAVE NEVER

The group sits in a circle of chairs. One player stands in the middle. The middle player says one thing he has never done. Anyone in a chair who has done this thing stands up and looks for a new chair that is open. The middle player tries to steal an open chair. Players cannot sit in the chair they've immediately left. The player who ends up in the middle gives a new "I have never..." statement.

Some common uses for this game in Writerly Play:
Characterization: Players make statements based on what their characters have never done. The game can be flipped so that the player uses the phrase "I like to..." rather than "I have never..." For young groups, "I like to..." is easier. Also, the game is easier for younger students if the players stand if they agree, rather than if they disagree.

Idea Generation: Players remember exciting, funny, or otherwise memorable life events through the "I have never..." ideas introduced in the game. These ideas then lead to interesting story material.

NAME VOLLEYBALL

Divide the players into two teams. There is an imaginary volleyball net in the middle of the room. Start play by giving an imaginary volleyball to one student, who fills it up with something goopy, such as chocolate pudding. (The volleyball unscrews in the middle so you can fill it up.) The players hit the volleyball over the net, calling the name of whomever they are sending the ball to. If a player holds the ball too long, say for more than five seconds, the ball explodes and the group hoses off the player (who is now covered in pudding) with imaginary hoses. Then, the player who has been hosed down chooses something new to put in the volleyball.

This is a good get-to-know-you game, and also a fun warm-up after a group knows one another.

MACHINE

Gather the players in an audience area and define the playing space. As a group, decide on the kind of machine you'd like to make. One player initiates the machine by moving into the playing space and starting a sound and motion which they can repeat. Players join the machine as quickly as they can until every group member is part of the machine. Then, the facilitator can use a dial to speed up and slow down the machine. Try improvising a story where one part of the machine is broken—how does the machine work now? Become the mechanic and fix the machine.

Variations

Challenge advanced players to speed up and slow down the machine on their own. First, they must speed up until they go so fast that they explode. But no player may move any faster than any other at any given time. Then, the machine must slow down together so that finally, at some point, everyone is frozen.

USE THAT OBJECT

This game is played in two teams of two. Each team gets one generic prop, such as a scarf or a broom. In this game we use real, physical objects, rather than imaginary ones. Each team gets the count of five to use their prop in a new way. A broom could become a hockey stick, a baseball bat, a battering ram, etc. Switch back and forth from team to team until one team runs out of ideas. When one team gets stuck, four new players begin a new round with new props.

WHAT ARE YOU DOING?

Begin standing. Player one asks player two, "What are you doing?" Player two states an action, such as, "Mopping the floor." Player one begins the action—in this case, mopping the floor—in mime. Then, player two asks, "What are you doing?" Player one, who is still mopping the floor, gives a completely different action as his or her answer, such as, "Eating spaghetti." Now, player two begins eating spaghetti. Player one stops mopping the floor to ask, "What are you doing?" The game can repeat until one player runs out of actions or repeats one that has already been named. Alternatively, the facilitator can freeze the game after the first players have played for thirty seconds to a minute, and then replace them with two new players. Quick substitutions keep the game moving and the rest of the class engaged.

WORD TOSS

Play sitting or standing. Player one tosses a small object to player two. As he tosses, he says a word. When player two catches the object, she tosses it back, adding a new word that is connected in some way. This game can also be played in a circle.

Some common uses for this game in Writerly Play:

Review Spelling: Each player spells a word on catching the object, and then gives a new word to the other player.

Develop Vocab: Add adjectives to nouns, or brainstorm alternate verbs for generic ones.

Build Storytelling Skills: Create a story one word or phrase at a time.

Tableau Games

Any moment frozen in time allows observers to see what might otherwise go unseen. Tableau games help writers make and revise choices. Tableau games also allow writers to focus on one moment in time and think specifically about just one thing. In one-on-one settings, these games can be adapted so that mentees create individual statues of specific story moments.

PORTRAITS

This game works best with groups of six. Have players line up at the back of the room. When the game begins, players run one at a time to the center of the room and strike a pose. As soon as each player joins the portrait, they must freeze. There are four rules.

1. There should be players on high, middle, and low levels.
2. Players need to be in contact with one other player in the group with a hand, foot, elbow, and so forth.
3. Players must hold their own weight, so there can be no leaning or pushing.
4. All faces in the portrait must be seen.

At first, see how fast the players can build a portrait and then return to the back of the room, ready to build a new one. After they've done this once or twice, give additional directions such as, "Make the tiniest portrait you can," or "Make the largest portrait you can." As the game continues, switch players and add new layers of complication with each round.

Some common uses for this game in Writerly Play:

Scene Building: Often used with a familiar story, this game can explore what belongs in the beginning, middle, and end of a story. Also, this game can explore a writer's choice of which scenes to show and which to summarize. As a performance game, Portraits is a strong way to introduce a discussion of climax and other nuanced writing concepts.

Revision: A writer might direct fellow players through a sequence of scenes, to get a more complete picture of her own story, to try out a few options for where the story might go, and to receive feedback.

Idea Generation: By building portraits of key life moments, players have the opportunity to remember their stories and generate ideas.

SCULPTURES

In partner pairs, players sculpt one another into characters from their stories. The sculptor shows his partner the physical position he'd like her to take on, and the partner mirrors with as much detail as possible. The sculptor should work from head to foot, giving small details as he goes. Deepen this game by having the sculptor try three possible positions that illustrate different emotions. Give both partners turns to be the sculptor.

Play standing. The facilitator provides prompts that guide the writers through a series of frozen pictures that show the progression of the story, important moment to important moment. With each "click," the writers move on to the next important moment of the story. This game works well with the addition of "rewind." Since a slideshow condenses the story into highlighted moments, writers can play through their stories once, then rewind. After a little time to reflect and/or discuss their ideas, they can play through the stories again with revisions.

In-the-Moment Games

In these games, players act as their characters in order to better understand how their character thinks, speaks, moves, and reacts.

A caution for these games: As writers take on the roles of characters in other writers' stories, the potential for difficulty arises. To avoid conflict, point out that nothing that happens in the games MUST happen in the eventual stories. Also, remind those players helping the authors that their roles are to be generic characters off which the others can react and learn. Their role is not to write the story. At times, you may need to stop the game and redirect. If the players are stuck, one great strategy is to pause and ask the audience what the player opposite the author might ask to help move the scene forward. This helps the audience learn how to be helpful and keeps the players on stage from feeling put on the spot.

ACT IT OUT

In this simple scene game, the writer acts out a moment in real time. Sometimes it helps to play out the moment with Slideshow first (described in the "Tableau Games" section) and then to act out the moment in real time. Sometimes it is helpful to have the writer narrate as she acts, and other times action without words is enough.

BAD, WORSE, WORST/ BIG, BIGGER, BIGGEST

First, ask the players to walk around the room as they normally do. Call "freeze." Do this a few times quickly using creative types of movement to transition into a playful state. Once the group has become involved in the game, ask the players to act out a moment from their stories.

With Bad, Worse, Worst, start with a problem. After playing out the moment, rewind and try it again with exaggeration. Then, try it again in its worst possible state. The goal here is to explore how terrible a conflict can become and raise the stakes.

With Big, Bigger, Biggest, start with any scene. After playing out the moment, rewind and try it again with exaggeration. Then, try it all-out in its most outlandish form. The goal here is to explore how to exaggerate the physicality or the specifics of the situation.

After playing out all three versions of the moment, ask the players to consider which one would work best for their stories. Gather a few ideas from the group to see what kinds of insight are developing, and to help players who are unsure develop ideas from those the group has offered.

BEST DAY/WORST DAY

In this game, the writer speaks from his or her character's point of view to describe the best possible day. Afterward, rewind and tell the worst possible day. This game works well played in partner pairs. In order to explore motivation and multiple perspectives, this game can also be played from the points of view of various characters in the story.

COMING HOME

Ask the players to move around the space in a variety of ways and then do a quick round of Character Layer (described in the "Movement Games" section). Once the players have "become" their characters, they should freeze. Ask the players to imagine they are standing at their front door. They are coming home after a long day. They should each reach forward, open their door, enter their house, and do whatever they might do as they come inside. This may include speaking to themselves, or staying silent. After they have gotten a good start, freeze them again. Then, have them continue one at a time, spotlighting each player to facilitate give and take among them. Switch when players get stuck, to give them time to think, or when they've been in the spotlight for a few moments. Keep the momentum moving between players. At the end of the game, ask the players to finish their scenes in unison. Give them 10 to 20 seconds to do so. Spotlighting (rather than letting the scenes play out independently) can help raise the level of play across the room and help you as facilitator see what's working.

DAILY TASKS

Move players around the space. Side-coach the players through Character Walk to help them transition into character. Then call freeze. Give them a situation their characters would encounter daily—for instance, making lunch, brushing their teeth, or packing their backpack. Ask the players to use imaginary objects to explore how their characters would do each task. If desired, coach the writers to speak their "inner thoughts" aloud. Vocalizing helps players find words that might eventually end up on the page.

Extend the game by trying some more important tasks, such as wrapping an important present or getting ready before a performance or speech.

GREETINGS

Use this game after a round of Character Walk. Ask the players to find another player, face that person and greet him or her in a particular way. Possibilities include:

- As though you hadn't seen them for years
- As though you know a secret about them
- As though they've just done something that you're angry about
- As though you're on your way to their surprise party
- As though you just realized you forgot to send them a thank-you note for a gift
- As though you forgot their name

HALF-TIME/ TIME WARP

Play standing. In this game, the players act out their stories in a set amount of time. The facilitator prompts through side-coaching to keep the story moving. I usually use the general stages of the Hero's Journey to guide players through the basic stages of a story, using questions such as, "If your character were to meet someone at this point who could provide insight, what would that moment look like? Where would it happen? What action would your character be taking?" The first time through, the story is timed, and it should take four to five minutes.

In Half-Time, the story must be told in half the time, but it should still contain action and dialogue and narration. Next, the writer tells the story again, half-timing the events again. The purpose of this game is to focus in on the important moments as the story becomes shorter and shorter.

With Time Warp, the writer should choose a small moment and use at least a minute to tell it. The second time through, they should extend the moment so it takes twice as long, adding detail and moment-to-moment action. Repeat as desired. Here, the goal is to expand summary into fully fleshed-out scenes.

INTERVIEW

Play sitting or standing. The writer plays the character he or she would like to explore. The facilitator plays a reporter or someone else who is interviewing the character. Ask questions to help the writer explore the character's motivations and his or her feelings about the experiences of the story. Extend the game by playing the game from the point of view of a few different characters in the story. Depending on your group, you might interview four or five players at a time as though they are on a panel or on different channels. Group interviews allow for spotlighting, so that players have time to think while others are speaking. This approach speeds up the game, and adds energy and fun. Also, with larger classes, interviewing groups helps offset the boredom that can develop as the audience members wait for their turn.

THREE-CHAIR CONVERSATION

Set out three chairs in a row. In the standard format of this game, the first chair is the "main character" chair. The player in this chair takes on the role of his or her main character. The middle chair is the interview chair. The facilitator usually sits in this chair to ask questions of the other players. The third chair is the "antagonist" chair. In this chair, the player takes on the role of the character who drives the conflict in his or her story. The goal here is to have players take on two contrasting characters in relatively rapid succession and for writers to get to know their characters better through the interview process. After every few questions, the players cycle through the chairs. The player in the first chair moves to the third chair, and someone from the audience cycles into the game. Rotate the players quickly so that everyone can play within a short amount of time—say, ten minutes at the most.

Scene Games

These scene games teach specific skills, and are often used to build skills without using the writer's story as source material. In one-on-one situations, improvisation games can be played between mentor and mentee. In this case, if the mentor is careful to let the writer drive the scene forward, the scene material can become the writer's story.

ADD AN OBJECT

Choose a location that appeals to many senses; for instance: candy shop, hair salon, bakery, backstage, farm, high school cafeteria. Alternate entering the location and describing a particular object. Shape the object in space and narrate to describe how it smells, tastes, looks, sounds, and feels. Then the next player enters and adds a new object. Every object that is created must remain, so no one can walk through an established shelf, for instance. Once the space is created, extend the game by playing Three Tries or another Scene game or In-the-Moment game in the setting. Explore using the objects and setting as part of the action.

ADJECTIVE SCENE

Write adjectives on index cards, one per card. Play standing. Spread the cards out around the space, face down. Begin the scene, and after a few moments, freeze and pick up a card. Add the quality of the adjective to everything you do. After a few more moments, switch cards again. Debrief by discussing what gestures, actions, tones of voice, or facial expressions fit well with each emotion/adjective. Sometimes playing this game silently helps the physicality become stronger.

ASIDES

Play standing. Begin a scene with a who, what, and where. At any point during the scene, either player can call freeze and share what they are really thinking as an aside. When the scene begins again, the players continue as though the subtext hasn't been revealed.

With three or more characters, the third and/or fourth player can provide the subtext. Challenge the subtext players to add drama to the scene, and the onstage characters to accept and run with what the subtext actors give them.

CHARACTER SCRAMBLE

Write names of larger-than-life characters on cards. For example, Alligator, Superman, Troll, or Princess. Scatter the cards around the playing space. Move around the space for a short countdown and then pick up cards. Alternate choosing a scenario—such as making cookies, or decorating for a party. Then, take thirty seconds to a minute to complete the scene. After the scene is done, drop the cards and move around the space again to find a new character. The goal is to explore the vast physical and vocal options for characters.

EXITS AND ENTRANCES

Begin standing. Each player chooses a common word, such as yes, no, go or please. Choose a who, what, and where. Choose an active scenario, allowing for many reasons to enter and exit the stage, such as fixing a broken-down car, decorating for a party, building a house, or preparing backstage before a play. All players start on stage. If a player's word is said, he or she must leave the stage, giving a reasonable explanation for their exit. He or she must enter when the word is said again.

FORTUNATELY, UNFORTUNATELY

Players stand facing one another. Begin the game with a statement, such as, "Grimy the Gremlin hadn't had a bath for days," and strike a pose. Then, the other player strikes a frozen pose and adds, "Fortunately, he was all brown and warty, so no one knew." The game continues until you've built to a climax and resolution.

Some common uses for this game in Writerly Play:

Skill Building: Players create a story that is unrelated to the writer's story.

Idea Generation: Players create ideas that might add to the writer's story.

FREEZE

Two players are given a specific scene; for instance, they are sisters baking cookies and suddenly a kitchen emergency happens. Once they reach their scene's climax, call freeze and send in a new player. The new player tags out a player and takes his or her exact position. Then, the two players begin an entirely new scene. If they're stuck, suggest that the players find an object between them and begin to use it together. As in all improvisational games, encourage the players to say yes to one another's ideas. If your class is advanced, challenge the audience to call freeze when they see a new scene possibility.

GIBBERISH TRANSLATION

Set up three chairs in a row. The two players in the outside chairs speak entirely separate made-up languages (gibberish). The player in the center chair is the translator. The player on the right is making a proposal to the player on the left; for example, inviting her on an exciting adventure or giving him a good job. They begin their conversation in small bits, and the translator puts whatever is said into English. The translator does his best to understand what is being said, but once he translates the gibberish into English, what he says goes. Rotate players through the seats, so each has the opportunity to be the translator and gibberish speaker.

KITTY WANTS A CORNER

Gather the players into a circle. One player—who is the kitty—stands in the middle. The kitty goes up to a player in the circle and says, "Kitty wants a corner." The other player replies, "Go see my next-door neighbor," and sends the kitty in one direction or the other. The kitty must go right up to the player whom they are asking, instead of yelling from the middle of the circle. Behind the kitty's back, the other players make eye contact and switch places with one another. The kitty tries to steal a place while it is vacant. Players must switch with another player—they can't run across the circle randomly.

Use this game to explore objectives and how characters may try to reach their objectives.

THREE TRIES

Begin standing. Choose a problem scenario with many physical possibilities, such as moving a bed out of an apartment and down a few flights of stairs, or fixing a flat tire in the jungle. The objective of this game is to try three solutions with true effort. Only the third solution works. This game helps develop the understanding of why three is a strong number when it comes to building stories.

QUESTIONS

In this game, the players may speak only in questions. The goal is to move the story forward using only questions. Start with a setting and a situation. Whenever a player runs out of questions, start over.

STAGE DIRECTIONS

This game is played with two players. One player begins the scene with a line of dialogue. The other player adds, "she said, and then slammed the door" (or another line of stage directions). Then player one acts out the directions. Player two adds a new line of dialogue, and then player one completes the line with stage directions; for instance, "he said, while carefully folding up his newspaper." The players should incorporate into their ongoing dialogue whatever mood is introduced into the scene through the stage directions. When the scene has concluded, play a new scene with two new players. Use this game to explore action tags for dialogue.

WHAT ARE WE WATCHING?

Break the students into groups of five and ask them to decide on an event to watch. Some common ones are a movie, a sporting event, a play or opera, or a news conference. Make sure they decide in detail what happens at their event. They will perform this scene, starting from entering the seating area, which tells a great deal about where they are. What are they eating? How do they enter the seats? Then, together they must watch and react to the event. We should be able to tell that it's a baseball game or a frightening movie, and we should be able to tell by the group's reactions whether the favored team won or if the group likes the movie. Ask the actual audience to share the details they noticed in the scene. Can they guess what the group was watching?

Use this game to explore body language and how to use action to move a story forward.

Storytelling Games

In these games, a writer tells a partner a small moment from his or her story, usually from the main character's point of view. If the character would use gesture or act things out, then the author should do this, too. These games work well in partner pairs, so they are easy to adapt for one-on-one situations.

IF/THEN

After large room movement, ask players to pair up. Play with cause and effect by passing a scene back and forth. One player says, "If..." and fills in the blank. The other player says, "Then..." and fills in the blank. Add to the fun of the game by acting out each moment.

Variation:
Suddenly: Each player adds a line to the story that begins with "Suddenly," passing it back and forth.

Extend this game by asking each writer to retell his or her story with an adjustment. For instance, the writer might tell the same moment from another character's point of view, or imagine that the other player is a character in the story (a parent, for instance) and tell the story the way he or she would tell it to that character. This is a great game to discuss subtext and what characters say and don't say. Depending on the ability of your writer to get into character, the physical actions that characters use when they are telling the truth, or not, can also be informative. The other player may ask questions, or not, based on their role in the game.

SENTENCE BY SENTENCE/SCENE BY SCENE

Play this game sitting or standing, depending on how much of the story you want to act out as you tell it. Each player tells a sentence or a scene and then passes it on to the other player. The story is built moment by moment in this way.

SWITCH-EM CHAIRS

Play this game in pairs or as an audience game. Each writer sits in one of two chairs, and each chair has a particular role. For instance, one chair is the short sentences chair and the other is the long sentences chair. After playing by the rules of one chair, the writer switches to the other and abides by those rules. The mentor can facilitate by asking questions or by prompting from an audience perspective.

APPENDIX
TWO

Conferring Topics

———————○———————

Use this list of topics to spark conferring conversations.

A COLLECTION OF TOPICS

Use this list as a jumping-off place for developing conversations with your young writers.

Character

- Generating character ideas
- Describing characters physically
- Developing a rounded character
- Introducing main characters
- Introducing secondary characters
- Making a character sympathetic
- Naming characters and locations
- Showing character through gesture

- Showing character through action
- Showing character through telling detail
- Developing internal conflict
- Developing character motivation
- Developing contrasting motivations
- Developing antagonist motivation
- Using authority characters
- Using informed characters
- Using trusted characters
- Expressing humor through secondary characters
- Expressing humor through exaggeration
- Expressing humor through surprise
- Developing interior monologue
- Using simile and metaphor for character
- Identifying character roles

Setting

- Using just-right words
- Building reality through sensory detail
- Using details to make mind pictures
- Choosing details effectively
- Building a believable story world

- Mapping the story world

- Using setting rules to create conflict

- Using setting to reveal character

- Using comfortable settings for character development

- Introducing uncomfortable settings to create conflict

- Using setting to create tone

- Using weather to create tone

- Using simile to enrich description

- Using metaphor to enrich description

- Describing setting through action

- Building obstacles into a setting

- Building surprise into a setting

Plot/Pacing

- Experimenting with beginnings

- Setting up the promise of the story

- Using first lines effectively

- Introducing who, what, and where in the beginning

- Using foreshadowing for anticipation

- Developing a story through scene and summary

- Expanding summary into scene

- Compressing scene into summary

- Using flashbacks
- Transitioning from scene to scene
- Developing pacing with chapters
- Using paragraphs for pacing
- Using character decisions to develop plot
- Listing important scenes to explore plot
- Using the rule of threes to build stories
- Storyboarding a plot
- Plotting a story with the story mountain
- Plotting a Hero's Journey
- Showing character growth through scenes
- A Purpose for each scene
- Slowing down to highlight the hot spot
- Highlighting character conflict in the murky middle
- Highlighting cause and effect in the murky middle
- Developing external events in the murky middle
- Developing internal tension in the murky middle
- Using discovery in the murky middle
- Using complication in the murky middle
- Using twists and turns in the murky middle
- Raising the stakes
- Developing a subplot
- Building to a climax

- Using moment to moment action in the climax
- Making the most of the moment your character gives up
- Resolving the story conflict
- Tying up Loose ends
- Experimenting with endings
- Using surprise endings
- Using reflective endings
- Using circular endings

Point of View/Voice

- Discovering the voice of the story
- Using active verbs
- Using concrete nouns
- Using first-person point of view
- Using third-person limited point of view
- Using omniscient point of view
- Using multiple perspective
- Using an intrusive narrator
- Using letters, email, or newspapers
- Using quotes or facts to provide context
- Sticking to the chosen point of view
- Using a character's voice

- Using repetition for effect

- Experimenting with symbolism

Dialogue

- Using talk bubbles to explore dialogue
- Creating character-specific dialogue
- Using Dialogue to provide exposition
- Compressing dialogue for pacing
- Using subtext in dialogue
- Punctuating dialogue
- Using action for dialogue tags
- Using simple dialogue tags

Theme

- Finding the heart of the story
- Using figurative language to highlight the theme
- Using symbolism to highlight the theme
- Revising to highlight the theme
- Using word choice to heighten theme

Nonfiction

- Using a question to hook a reader
- Using a fact to hook a reader
- Using an image to hook a reader
- Using a compelling idea to hook a reader
- Developing a strong thesis statement
- Bridging between a hook and a thesis
- Defining three categories for an essay
- Creating an opening for the conclusion
- Restating the thesis in the conclusion
- Summing up thinking in the conclusion

Mechanics

- Crafting a title
- Cutting clutter from sentences
- Varying sentence length
- Combining short sentences
- Splitting long sentences
- Separating ideas into paragraphs
- Using Transitions effectively
- Avoiding the vague it/that

- Creating a complete sentence
- Using commas in simple sentences
- Using commas in complex sentences
- Using semicolons
- Using colons
- Using apostrophes
- Using dashes
- Using end punctuation
- Using conjunctions to combine phrases
- Using conjunctions to create relationships
- Using conjunctions to link sentence elements
- Using conjunctions to clarify time
- Moving misplaced modifiers
- Moving misplaced phrases
- Using homophones: they're, their, there
- Using homophones: two, too, to
- Using it's and its